The Grinnell Beowulf

The Grinnell Beowulf

A Translation with Notes

Timothy D. Arner, Eva Dawson, Emily Johnson,
Jeanette Miller, Logan Shearer, Aniela Wendt, and Kate Whitman

Illustrations by Caleb Neubauer

The Grinnell Beowulf

By Timothy D. Arner, Eva Dawson, Emily Johnson, Jeanette Miller, Logan Shearer, Aniela Wendt, and Kate Whitman with illustrations by Caleb Neubauer

Published by Grinnell College
 1115 Eighth Ave.
 Grinnell, IA 50112

Simultaneously published in digital form by Digital Grinnell:
 http://digital.grinnell.edu/

Related material available at thegrinnellbeowulf.com

secg eft ongan
sið Beowulfes   snyttrum styrian
ond on sped wrecan   spel gerade,
wordum wrixlan.

(871-74)

Professor's Introduction

     Beowulf is a poem about a man who fights a dragon just to get a glimpse of an ancient treasure. Like the gold in the dragon's barrow, the text of *Beowulf* remained hidden away for hundreds of years. The manuscript simply existed, unnoticed and unread, until 1805, when a Danish historian named Grímur Thorkelín published a copy of the text, letting the world know that there was a new hoard to be uncovered. It was J.R.R. Tolkien who truly woke the dragon with his 1936 essay "*Beowulf*: The Monsters and the Critics," unleashing a terrifying and spectacular flame upon the study of English literary history. For many years since, scholars have confronted the great beast of Old English literature, attempting to solve its riddles, explain its oddities, and conquer its cruxes. The poem resists such advances, refusing to surrender itself to any simple explanations or clear articulations of its meaning. Countless high school and undergraduate students have felt themselves scorched by its flames, but so have accomplished critics and translators, facing many desperate moments when it seemed the battle for clarity and explication was unwinnable. Those who watch such quests from afar, the unconverted who see *Beowulf* not as treasure but as a dusty relic from a distant past, will usually ask, "Why would anybody want to fight a dragon in the first place?"

     In creating *The Grinnell Beowulf*, our goal was not to slay the dragon but to tame it. That is, we didn't want to reduce the poem to a simpler form but instead to produce a translation and edition that would allow readers to find pleasure in the poem's complexity. Literal translations that keep the poem's form and render Old English words using modern equivalents allow readers to see how each line of the poem functions but not necessarily how the pieces fit together into a graceful and fluid whole. We tried to find a middle ground by carefully maintaining a fidelity to the original text while using idiomatic English and free verse to communicate our best sense of the *Beowulf*-poet's intention. As a poem that used the then-current language of Anglo-Saxon England to offer a nostalgic glimpse of a legendary past, *Beowulf* was always both old and new. We wanted our translation to feel the same: ancient and strange but also vibrant and relevant. *The Grinnell Beowulf* is an invitation to better understand Beowulf's world by making it feel as if it is part of our own.

This translation differs from others in a number of respects. This is the first version produced by undergraduate students for an undergraduate audience. Hopefully to the benefit of the poem (and certainly to their own benefit), the students were learning about *Beowulf* and the Old English language through the process of translation, which meant that nothing had been predetermined and everything evolved as ongoing discovery. Working as a group in which each line was constructed, evaluated, and revised by the seven of us, we translated and composed by committee, working toward unity rather than privileging an individual voice. While most other published translations of *Beowulf* were produced by men, we had two men and five women involved in the discussion. Throughout the process, we knew we were creating a translation and edition for use in an undergraduate classroom. I was making an edition for my students; my students were making an edition for their peers.

The students involved in this project have performed extraordinary feats. They each brought their own particular set of skills and interests. Some had done extensive language study and had taken courses in linguistics, others had taken classes and seminars on the craft of poetry. They immersed themselves in the painstaking process of recording the meaning and grammatical function of each Old English word and then slowly constructing accurate sentences. Our classroom became a library full of scholarship and editions to be consulted when help was needed. Along the way, the students honed their research skills as they studied medieval culture and waded into the wondrous landscape of *Beowulf* scholarship. The translation process, moving from Old English to modern English and then from sentences to poetry, became an intensive boot camp in close reading. They learned how to present at a scholarly conference; they taught themselves book design. When it came time to face the dragon, these students were not cowardly retainers. Eva, Emily, Logan, Jeanette, Aniela, Kate – these are all Wiglafs.

But that doesn't make me this group's Beowulf. I'm not even an Anglo-Saxonist. I had worked with Old English in graduate school, taking a seminar on *Beowulf* and co-authoring an article on the Anglo-Saxon poem *Christ III*, but my recent work focuses on later medieval literature. I proposed a Mentored Advanced Project on *Beowulf* because I wanted to improve my teaching of English Historical Linguistics and I thought it would provide new avenues for research. It certainly has served both those purposes. Yet, when I considered the six students who volunteered to spend their summer working through *Beowulf*, I knew that we had an opportunity to produce something that would do more than this, that would last beyond August. If these students were going to acquire the skills and knowledge needed to work with *Beowulf*, they would need to work as a team and do research on various aspects of the poem. If they were going to do all that research, they could write brief annotations to help explain its language and themes. And if we were able to produce a readable and interesting new translation accompanied by helpful notes, we could share our work with a larger community.

The project certainly has lasted beyond the summer of 2012. Before we started work, I put together a schedule that would allow us to get through the whole poem. The students would work in pairs to translate 100 lines every few days, getting through 600 lines per week. The plan was for the full group to meet with me twice a week to work through the literal translation of the lines, checking for accuracy and rendering them into our own poetic form and language. If everyone was prepared and we moved quickly, we could get through the whole poem in eight weeks. During our first two-hour meeting, we got though the first 12 lines. At our next meeting, another 20. Eventually, as the students became more familiar with the language, and as my own reading of Old English improved, we were able to move faster. The literal translations became more accurate, and we were lucky to quickly establish our own poetic sensibility and narrative voice. The collaborative nature of the project meant that, at times, we had not just six students but seven teachers in the room, each with a unique perspective but a shared goal.

We spent a lot of time discussing Old English grammar and poetic conventions, making sure that everyone understood which subject went with which verb and each object. If there was a question about the original text, we would look at images of the manuscript. Once we made sure a set of lines was accurate, we considered different ways to make it read well as modern poetry. Each line was carefully considered and debated amongst the group; we didn't move on until everyone was satisfied. We read back over each section numerous times to make sure that the narrative flowed and the beauty of the original was conveyed. Meetings became longer and more frequent. We would meet first thing in the morning, pick up lunch from the appropriately-named Dragon Wagon across the street from campus, and then work through the afternoon. At night, the students would do more of the literal translation in preparation for the following day's meeting. By the end of the summer, we had translated all of *Beowulf* into a readable, and at times quite beautiful, poem of our own.

Work continued through the next year, long after the summer stipends had been spent. We wrote and revised annotations for each line that we felt needed further explanation. I wanted to provide notes that would help a first-time reader understand the complex world of the poem or help direct advanced students doing research of their own. I also wanted to justify our translation choices and explain how we had made decisions about particularly difficult and ambiguous lines. We continued to revise our poem, arguing about words, phrases, line breaks. We read and discussed scholarship that could help us reach the best possible conclusions about the poem's really tricky moments. Is the bad queen's name Modthryth, Thrytho, or Fremu? What exactly is an "ale-shower"? Does Beowulf get cursed by the gold? Is there a better word than *Hwæt*? We had to work in fits and starts as the students focused on coursework and spent time abroad, and as I taught and worked on other scholarship. But as the project moved along, and as we saw the incredible images Caleb Neubauer was producing for our edition, we found the energy and the *ofermod* to make sure that we put together an edition worthy of the name *Beowulf*.

My role has been to lead and to listen, to manage the group and be part of the team. Because this would only succeed if everyone was truly invested, I tried to share my expertise while having the group each consensus rather than simply follow direction. Everyone's unique perspective and the poem's tricky ambiguities led to impassioned arguments over what a passage means or should sound like. For all the times I felt myself frustrated by not having the group see things my way, these discussions ultimately led to productive outcomes, in terms of both understanding the original poem and crafting our translation. It has been a long, difficult, frustrating, and immensely rewarding experience. It has been transformative, shaping the way I understand my role as a teacher-scholar and demonstrating new ways in which serious work can be done with student collaboration. As we reach the end, I could not be more proud as I gaze upon our hoard and invite you to share in it. It was a battle, and I'm happy not to have been mortally wounded in the process.

We wanted to honor the institution that allowed us to do this project by calling our edition *The Grinnell Beowulf.* This edition represents, I think, a model of how teaching and research work in tandem in a liberal arts college and how undergraduate students can collaborate with faculty to produce scholarship in the humanities. We want the poem to be able to stand on its own as a work of translation and creative writing, and we have included notes and introductory matter designed to encourage further inquiry into a range of scholarly fields. This is the edition that I always wanted to have when teaching *Beowulf* in my courses. For students, this edition is designed to suit your needs whether you're reading Anglo-Saxon poetry for the first time or delving into this *word-hord* once again in an upper-level seminar. For teachers, we want the edition to foster classroom discussion on a variety of levels. For all readers, we hope that you'll find our *Beowulf* to be as exciting, heartbreaking, and intellectually stimulating as the Anglo-Saxon audience must have found theirs.

Timothy D. Arner

Students' Introduction

The birth and breadth of this project were both unexpected. During a Traditions of English Literature course, Professor Arner made an offhand comment about translating *Beowulf* as a Mentored Advanced Project, or MAP. At Grinnell, a MAP involves students working with a professor to conduct research in a focused area of study for a summer or a semester. Professor Arner sent out an email to all students in this class to gauge the interest in such a project. Six affirmative responses later, the *Beowulf* group was formed. While the academic year requires dividing time between various courses and activities, we liked the idea of dedicating a summer to a singular topic. At first, the six of us thought we were signing up for an exercise in translation, an introduction to the language of *Beowulf*. Before we started, Professor Arner suggested the possibility of using this project to produce an edition of the poem. Ambitious, eager, and completely naïve, we quickly agreed, not yet understanding what we had gotten ourselves into.

Collectively, we had taken a variety of courses that contributed to our preparation for and development of the project. We are five English majors and one sociology major. Our literature classes provided us ample experience with close reading. Some of us had taken courses in linguistics and creative writing, and we all had studied a foreign language. Many of us had studied synthetic languages like Latin, German, and Russian, so grammatical structures foreign to modern English were familiar to us. All of us had read *Beowulf* before, though none of us imagined it would become such a huge part of our lives.

While we were equipped with relevant experiences and abilities, we had to generate an original system in order to execute this project. Trial and error defined our experiences for much of the first few weeks. We were constantly making mistakes and reinventing our system. Eventually we developed a method that worked. Since we were just learning Old English, it was necessary to look up, consider, and debate every single word in *Beowulf*. We did just that, entering every word in a massive spreadsheet complete with definitions and grammatical functions. We returned to this database to check and recheck grammar, and we consulted other translations to check and recheck meaning. Engaging with the same 3,182 lines for months, we could not imagine a more immersive experience. Our own *Beowulf* began to take shape, slowly and sometimes painfully. We debated prepositions, scoured our thesauruses for the perfect word, and dedicated entire meetings to capitalization or line breaks. This attention to detail often led to frustration, and in those times the poem itself became a mediator. An exemplary moment came in the *Finn saga*, a seeming digression full of odd syntax and complicated political relations, the beauty of which renewed our enthusiasm:

> The woman lamented with a song of mourning.
> The warrior was lifted.
> The greatest of funeral fires spiraled
> to the clouds, roaring above the barrow,
> heads consumed by flames,
> gashes burst open and blood
> streamed forth from the body's scars.
> The flame, greediest of ghosts,
> swallowed all those who had fallen
> there in war, men of both nations.
> Their glory had passed away.

The poem manages to weave the grotesque with the beautiful, the tragic with the majestic. After reading aloud a passage like this, there would often be an audible sigh from our group, a vocal recognition of the poem's deeply affective nature. The original poem is inherently inspiring, but it demanded a considerable amount of effort to extract and render its beauty into our own *Beowulf*.

Our summer of *Beowulf* challenged us to become active agents in the learning process. Creating a classroom edition of *Beowulf* allowed us to understand how professional scholarship is produced. We frequently encounter scholarship, translations, and criticism in our academic lives, but this project gave us the unique opportunity to be involved in the sort of work that we had previously taken for granted. Additionally, we worked alongside a professor and learned to emulate his research process while developing our own. When confronted with a profusion of books and articles to read through and analyze, we were able to ask Professor Arner how he would approach it, rather than how we should approach it. We were not serving as research assistants to a professor for his own project, nor were we submitting lines of translation in exchange for a grade. Professor Arner facilitated and grounded the project, but every member had equal say. Creating *Beowulf* was an entirely collaborative undertaking; we all learned from and taught one another.

Having seven contributors enabled us to conduct a significant amount of research in specific areas of the text, each of us attempting to develop expert knowledge of a facet of *Beowulf*. We had an opportunity to do extensive research on a series of narrow yet interrelated topics and apply it to our creative process as an enhancement rather than a crutch. During meetings we would surround ourselves with various translations, and we engaged in conversation with them as we produced our own edition. While the humanities typically values independent work, this project enabled us to build a scholarly community in which we both critiqued and supported one another. Each member proved essential to the group dynamic. It is unusual for a group to translate a text, and for good reason. For many decisions, we had to reconcile differing opinions. *Beowulf* required many long hours together, wading through tricky passages and battling for preferred words. However, our collaboration also meant that we could accomplish a great deal in a relatively short period of time. We had to trust one another to complete the tasks necessary for the next meeting, to do the research to support our claims, and to offer an informed perspective on the text.

None of us had ever spent this much time with a single text. Before we started this translation *Beowulf* was barely more than an oddly-constructed monster story to us. One would think that after poring over every single word in the poem over the course of a year and a half, we would have tired of it. However, *Beowulf* still surprises us by revealing new facets of itself. The way we interpreted and related to the story changed as well. Every time we learned more about Finn or re-read a passage that at first seemed nonsensical, we appreciated the complex craft of the poem more. Every day was filled with multiple levels of discovery. Phrases in which Old and modern English did not seem that different, like *grim gæst Grendel* ("the grim guest Grendel"), made us feel like we understood and could connect to the language. A bit of research might reveal a new emotional aspect of the poem: understanding the function of *wergild* (monetary compensation for murder) makes it so much more tragic when a warrior accidentally kills his own brother. Seven different opinions and research areas allowed us to scrutinize different aspects of the text. Nothing was unexamined, and that is how we think *Beowulf* is best read: with patience, commitment, and a rabid attention to detail.

When asked to name a favorite book or poem, few people would likely answer *Beowulf*. On the surface, it seems unnecessarily complicated and very foreign. A first reading hardly allows a reader to draw connections or sympathize with the characters. Tension builds and then is diffused by interruptive "digressions." *Beowulf* is not an easy read. It is, however, an extraordinarily rewarding reading experience that takes work and attention but responds to the reader's efforts in kind. The reader can easily appreciate the gore of battle and glory of heroism that characterize the poem. However, when read with care, the poem also offers profound depictions of tragedy and loss, becoming even more powerful in its quieter moments.

This poem means the world to us. As a group of seniors looking back on a project that began just after our sophomore year, we have found that this poem has completely shaped our educational experiences and academic identities. We feel incredibly lucky and grateful to have had this opportunity. This poem was a gift, and none of us can imagine what our college careers would have been like without *Beowulf*. We offer this gift to others in the hope that they can appreciate the brilliance of *Beowulf* as we do.

Eva, Emily, Jeanette, Logan, Aniela, and Kate
October 2013

Note on Translation

We referred to both *Klaeber's Beowulf*, 4th edition and Mitchell and Robinson's *Beowulf: An Introduction*, which present the entirety of the Old English text, glossaries with semantic and grammatical information about each word, and extensive notes with contextual information about the world of the poem. Additionally, we consulted images of the original manuscript using the *Electronic Beowulf* CD-ROM (now available online at http://ebeowulf.uky.edu/) to evaluate damaged sections of the text and the emendations suggested by modern editors.

Using these two editions of *Beowulf* as base texts, the group created a spreadsheet to document the meaning and grammatical information for each word in the poem. Then students worked in pairs to construct a literal estimate of the translation: a preliminary draft that maintained the grammar and vocabulary employed by the Old English text. We created online Google documents that everyone could access and edit simultaneously in real time. The group as a whole, including Professor Arner, met regularly to share segments of literal translation to ensure that the narrative sense of the lines was clear. In places where we were uncertain about how to render the literal translation, we referred to the work of other translators: Howell D. Chickering, Jr.'s *Beowulf: A Dual-Language Edition*, Seamus Heaney's *Beowulf*, and E.L. Risden's: *Beowulf: A Student's Edition*. Once we determined the basic meaning of a set of lines, we worked as a group to render our literal translation more poetically. Our goal was to allow each line of our poem to function as a relatively complete unit while maintaining lyric fluidity. Ultimately, we wanted to produce contemporary-sounding, readable poetry that remained as faithful as possible to the Old English text.

When we encountered difficult or ambiguous passages, or disagreement between translations, which was not uncommon, we consulted relevant scholarship. Each student selected an area of research: monsters, gender, Anglo-Saxon cultural practices, paganism and Christianity, English and Scandinavian analogues, and conflicting textual issues in the manuscript and various editions of the poem. The extensive commentaries included in *Klaeber 4*, Mitchell and Robinson's

Beowulf, and Chickering's *Beowulf* provided overviews of debates about difficult passages. Using a variety of scholarly resources to gain a clear sense of the poem's text and context, we made sure that each translation decision was informed by historical research and current trends in literary and textual criticism. Our edition includes notes that explain our decisions and, where appropriate, acknowledges alternative suggestions for how a passage might be understood.

In an effort to produce an idiomatic and accessible translation, we allowed ourselves to manipulate the poem's syntax. As an analytic language, modern English relies on word order (usually subject, verb, object) to convey meaning. Old English, however, is a synthetic language, which uses different forms of individual words to indicate each word's grammatical function in the sentence. Ultimately, this allows the Old English poet more liberty in the construction of each line. Because word order is less important, it is not uncommon to see a verb at the end of a clause. The passage that follows, because of its syntactic difference from modern English, required a rearrangement of word order:

> *þær him nænig wæter   wihte ne sceþede*
> *ne him for hrofsele   hrinan ne mehte*
> *færgripe flodes*

> [There, to him, no water in any way could do harm, nor him, because of the roofed hall, could not reach, the sudden grip of the flood.]

Our translation:

> No water harmed him in any way
> because of the hall's roof;
> the sudden rush of the flood could not reach him.

Old English poetry includes frequent variation, which is the restatement of terms and phrases within a passage. The flexibility of word order in Old English allows for this restatement to occur in the middle of sentences, as the following example shows:

> Beowulf maþelode,   bearn Ecgþeowes:
> "Geþenc nu, se mæra   maga Healfdenes,
> snottra fengel,   nu ic eom siðes fus,
> gold-wine gumena,   hwæt wit geo spræcon..."

[Beowulf spoke, son of Ecgtheow: "Remember now, famed kinsman of Healfdane, wise prince, now that I am eager for this expedition, gold friend of men, what we two formerly spoke of..."]

The various titles for Hrothgar both balance the poetic lines and emphasize the king's esteem. In most instances, we preserved variation but grouped the phrases together to give our own poem a sense of flow rather than disruption. We rendered the lines quoted above:

> The son of Ecgtheow spoke:
> "Hrothgar, renowned son of Healfdane,
> wise king and gold-friend of men,
> now that I am ready for this undertaking,
> remember what we two spoke of before."

In some places, we omitted repetitive phrases that interrupted the poem's flow or readability. At times, we replaced pronouns or titles with proper names to minimize confusion.

Old English poetry was composed in alliterative verse. Each line consists of two short half-lines separated by a space called a caesura. Each half-line contains two feet marked by one stressed syllable, complemented by one or two unstressed syllables. Within a line of alliterative verse, the first half-line, known as the a-verse, is linked to the second half-line, the b-verse, with the repetition of consonant or vowel sounds. In the following example, note the alliteration of "g" and "s" in each half-line:

Þa wæs eft hraðe
gearo gyrn-wræce   Grendeles modor,
siðode sorh-ful;   sunu deað fornam,
wig-hete Wedra.

While some translations preserve the alliterative verse, we chose not to imitate this structure. Instead, we used a more idiomatic free verse to allow for a more contemporary cadence and flow:

> The mother of Grendel was ready for vengeance,
> so she made a sorrow-bringing journey; death
> had destroyed her son in battle with the Geats.

We employed alliteration only when it aligned aesthetically with the natural, colloquial sound of the poem. This freedom meant that we could utilize alliteration in the phrase "death had destroyed her son" and maintain flow without trying to force more words to alliterate, or even keep the alliteration on the same line.

In a few cases, we employed Old English terminology and poetic devices where we felt they would be helpful and nondisruptive. For example, the word "thane" is a now-archaic descendent of *þegn/thegn* and it applies to a particular class of nobleman in Anglo-Saxon culture. In our translation, we appropriate the term to refer only to Beowulf so that our poem can clearly distinguish him from other warriors and noblemen. We also reproduce the original poem's use of kennings. A kenning is a compound word that links two nouns together to produce a metaphor for a different noun. For example, the kenning "whale-road" describes the ocean and "bone-house" alludes to the human body. Kennings are a distinctive feature of Old English poetry that we, along with most other translators, chose to preserve.

There are two words we felt could not be translated and still maintain their symbolic and poetic meanings: *Hwæt* and *scop*. *Hwæt* functions as an Anglo-Saxon call to attention, and we have left this word as it originally appears at the beginning of the poem and in a few places where it is used as a salutation. We chose to keep the word to provide a sense of the sound of Old English poetry and to signal important moments in the text. The second word we did not translate into modern terms is *scop*. A *scop* is an Anglo-Saxon poet, one who might compose original works or perform songs that had been passed down through oral tradition. The word *scop* comes from the Old English word for "to shape," and it reveals how the Anglo-Saxons thought about artistic composition. Just as a builder would "shape" a house (or how one Old English poem, *Cædmon's Hymn*, describes God "shaping" the world), the Anglo-Saxon *scop* was one who "shaped" a poem out of his available materials: the Old English lexicon, literary conventions, and cultural knowledge.

Translation requires continuously engaging and re-engaging the original text; the role of the translator is less to compose than to capture. As we revised over the course of a year and a half, we worked both with the original text and with our own, deepening our understanding of *Beowulf* and trying to find the most elegant way to convey that understanding. The more we returned to the text, the more we appreciated its technical and emotional brilliance and the harder we worked to preserve its beauty.

What is Beowulf?

Beowulf is an Anglo-Saxon poem likely composed between 700 and 1000 C.E. Few details are available concerning how the poem was conceived and in what forms it initially appeared. Though it was long believed to have originated as oral poetry, recent scholarship tends to focus on its function as a written text. *Beowulf* survives in only one manuscript, compiled in Britain around 1000 C.E., which also includes four other Anglo-Saxon texts. In 1731, a fire broke out in the private collection where the manuscript was being housed. Some of the pages were badly damaged, but, fortunately, the majority of the poem survived unharmed. The poem was transcribed in the 1780s, and these copies preserve bits of the text that have since been lost due to the fragile state of the original manuscript.

Beowulf tells the story of a man who performs a series of heroic feats, chronicling his victories over both humans and monsters. While best known for defeating terrifying creatures, Beowulf is no less skilled at navigating his world's complicated political landscape. The poem offers a glimpse into the social world of Anglo-Saxon England, which was organized around fealty to one's lord or king. Much of the poem takes place in the mead-hall, where the community gathered to feast, share stories, and participate in the ritualized distribution of treasure. Prestige and wealth were earned in battle, and the poem, on one level, celebrates the Anglo-Saxon warrior ethos and the social dynamic that reinforces this code.

Beowulf occupies a unique place in English literary history. Though now celebrated as a foundational text in the English canon, the poem would not have been known by other early English authors like Chaucer, Shakespeare, and Milton. After the text was first published in 1805, *Beowulf* was primarily valued as a historical document because characters and events described in the poem have analogues in Scandinavian, Germanic, Danish, and English chronicles. Attitudes toward the poem changed with the publication of J.R.R. Tolkien's landmark 1936 essay "*Beowulf*: The Monsters and the Critics," which argued that *Beowulf* functions as a unified and complex piece of literary

xpression. Perhaps its greatest influence has been in the twentieth
entury, notably on Tolkien's *Lord of the Rings* series, which established
he modern fantasy genre. Today, the poem plays an important role
n high school and undergraduate English curricula where it is often
resented as the first great English epic. For students and scholars who
tudy England's Anglo-Saxon era, *Beowulf* functions as the period's
terary masterpiece. The poem's length and complexity invite a wide
ange of critical approaches and interpretations, providing rich fodder
or research and scholarly debate about how to best understand the
spects of Anglo-Saxon culture revealed through the poem's language,
tructure, allusions, and narrative.

Although the poem is set in Scandinavia and parts of northern
urope, it is distinctly English, not only in its language but also in its
hemes. Germanic tribes, including the Angles, Saxons, and Jutes,
egan to migrate to Britain in the fifth century, where they established
utonomous kingdoms throughout the island. These kingdoms began
o unite in order to confront Danish and Scandinavian raiders, who
illaged lands along the eastern coastline before establishing permanent
ettlements in the eighth and ninth centuries. *Beowulf* uses the Old
nglish language to represent various aspects of Germanic, Danish,
nd Scandinavian culture and conflict and to articulate the values and
oncerns of the people who inhabited medieval Britain in the first
nillennium. The valuing of individual honor and loyal service to one's
ord were essential for the survival and prosperity of any particular group
r kingdom. Despite the perpetual threat of violence and war, the Anglo-
axons fostered a sense of community through artistic expression. Using
heir local Old English dialects, they composed and performed complex
oetry based on legendary, historical, and Biblical narratives. *Beowulf*
vould have felt to its original audience as it seems to us today: both
oreign and familiar.

The intermingling of Scandinavian mythology with
udeo-Christian theology in *Beowulf* reflects the gradual conversion of
he Anglo-Saxons to Christianity throughout the early Middle Ages.
'ope Gregory I sent missionaries to England in 597, and over the next
ew centuries the Anglo-Saxons developed their own particular brand of

Christianity that incorporated traditional beliefs and cultural practices carried over from northern Europe. Whether the Christian moments in the poem were always present or whether they were later added by monks who copied the text, they contribute to the poem's rich textual fabric by locating Grendel and his mother within both secular and sacred history. Both the poet and the characters within the poem pay homage to a single god, the Lord of All, and the poet provides moral commentary that seems to direct the audience toward living a moral life according to Christian principles. There is something uneasy in the poem's Christianity, however, as the poem never mentions Christ and refers only to events from the Old Testament. While some readings posit an analogy between Beowulf's death and Christ's passion, these must ignore the larger context and final result of the hero's sacrifice. Christianity is part of the world of the poem but it is not at its center.

Feuds and monsters are the central conflicts of the poem. For many readers, *Beowulf* is about the hero's battles against legendary adversaries: Grendel, Grendel's mother, and the dragon. These scenes of single-combat provide the main action and tension of the poem, but there are two things a reader must keep in mind in order to appreciate their full significance. First, the poem's hero is often described to be just as monstrous as the creatures he fights. The poem's language conflates Beowulf and his opponents during their conflicts, blurring the lines between human and inhuman, hero and monster. Second, the monsters participate in the ongoing cycle of feuds that *Beowulf* presents as its main subject. Grendel, his mother, and the dragon attack the Danes and Geats because they feel that they have been wronged, and the poem acknowledges their right to seek retribution. Throughout the poem, there are references to a number of other feuds between individuals and kingdoms, which operate according to the same principles. For some readers, the conflicts between human communities seem to be "digressions" from the poem's real subject, Beowulf's fights against monsters. For others, the poem's focus on monster fights distracts from the serious matter of Danish and Scandinavian history. It is clear, however, that all of the familial and political conflicts recounted in the poem provide a perspective for understanding the monster fights, and vice versa. In a work as tightly structured and thematically consistent as *Beowulf*, there are no digressions.

    Beowulf offers a warning against retributive violence. Vengeance operates according to the principle that one violent act should be answered with another, but *Beowulf* reveals the flaws in this system. In the fantasy world, a single hero can fight a monster or slay a dragon to save his people from the creatures feared to lurk in the shadows. In the world of human history, no hero can solve every problem with a well-forged sword or the strength of his handgrip. Beowulf can eliminate the threats posed by Grendel and his mother, but he cannot save the Danes from themselves. Beowulf can battle the dragon, but this only really serves to ensure the annihilation of the Geats by their human enemies. In each of the poem's various feuds, every victory is short-lived and every resolution doomed to failure. The poem revels in its depictions of bloodshed but lingers in its solemn meditations on loss. For every one of the poem's boasts and feasts, there is a lament and a funeral. What we ultimately learn from *Beowulf* is that the hero must understand not only when to pick up his sword, but, more importantly, when to put it down.

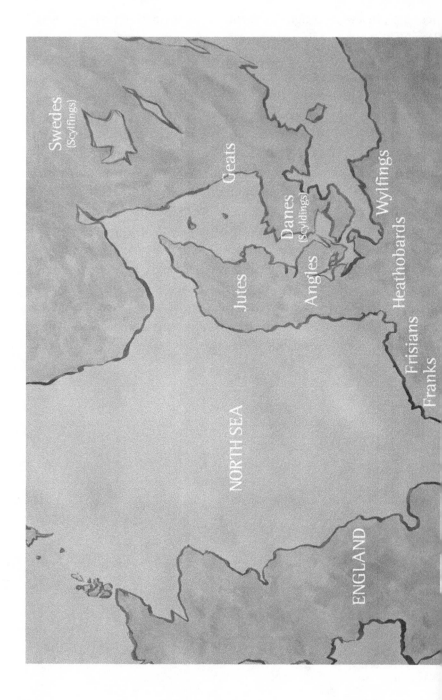

Timeline of Events in *Beowulf*

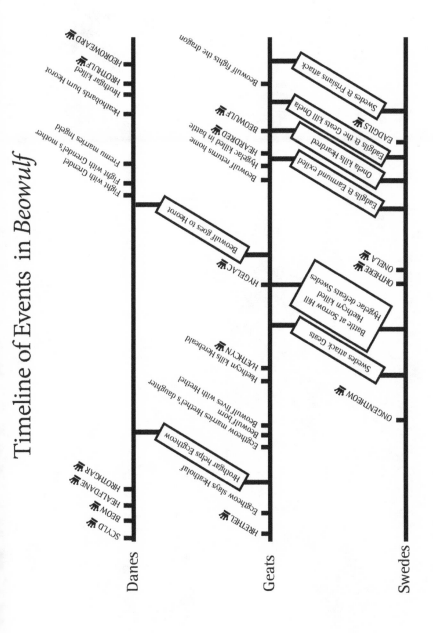

Danes

SCYLD
BEOW
HEALFDANE
HROTHGAR

Egtheow slays Heatholaf
Hrothgar helps Egtheow

Egtheow marries Hrethel's daughter
Beowulf born
Beowulf lives with Hrethel

Hethcyn kills Herebeald

Beowulf goes to Heorot

Fight with Grendel
Fight with Grendel's mother
Freru marries Ingeld

Heathobards burn Heorot
Hrothgar killed
HROTHULF
HEOROWEARD

Geats

HRETHEL

HYGELAC

Beowulf returns home
Hygelac killed in battle
HEARDRED

BEOWULF

Beowulf fights the dragon

Swedes

ONGENTHEOW

Swedes attack Geats

Battle at Sorrow Hill
Herthcyn killed
Hygelac defeats Swedes

OHTHERE
ONELA

Eadgils & Eanmund exiled
Onela kills Heardred
Eadgils & the Geats kill Onela

EADGILS

Swedes & Frisians attack

The Grinnell Beowulf

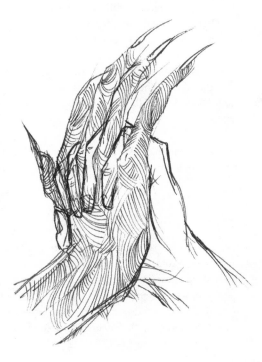

The first word of the poem is an Anglo-Saxon call to attention and a conventional opening to a formal speech or performance. It has been rendered variously as "Hark," "Listen," or "So." Since few modern English equivalents can adequately express the word's meaning while retaining its linguistic effect, we chose to keep *Hwæt* as a powerful but unobtrusive bit of Old English in our own poem.

4 The names of characters in *Beowulf* often indicate their nature or significance. Scyld becomes modern English "shield," while Scefing contains modern "sheaf," which reflects the agricultural nature of his society. Thus, his name signifies his role as king: both protector and provider for his people.

7 Scyld's story parallels both the Scandinavian myth of the swan knight and the Old Testament story of Moses. Both feature a child sent alone across water who grew up to lead a people. Despite his mythical beginnings, Scyld was regarded by the Danes as the historical ancestor of a noble bloodline.

11 "Whale-road" (*hron-rade*) is a kenning for the sea. Kennings are two-word phrases used figuratively, often as metaphors, in Old English and Norse poetry. Other examples include "bone-house" (body), "sword-gore" (blood), and "sky-candle" (sun).

17 This is not the poem's eponymous hero but rather another celebrated Scandinavian king. Even the poem's scribe seems to have confused the two, rendering Beow as "Beowulf."

25 This is the first of many sententious statements that appear throughout the poem. The poet or a character will sometimes pause the narrative to deliver a statement of moral commentary, known as a maxim or a gnome. As James Thayer explains, "The gnomic statements of accepted wisdom regarding the state of the cosmos and the proper conduct of men and women on earth serve as a foil for the steady stream of chaotic transformation in the poem as a whole and very often for the narrative action to which they are juxtaposed." See Thayer's essay, "Fractured Wisdom: The Gnomes of *Beowulf*."

Publication information for books and articles cited in the notes can be found in the bibliography at the back of the edition. *Klaeber 4* refers to *Klaeber's Beowulf*, 4th Edition. We use Chickering to refer to his *Beowulf: A Dual Language Edition.*

Corresponding line numbers for the original text appear in brackets.

Hwæt,

      We remember the Spear-Danes,
      glorious kings of people in days of yore,
      how these warriors fought courageously.
      Scyld Scefing* and his troops deprived
      many nations of their mead-halls
      and struck fear in the hearts of their noblemen.
      Though early in life his lineage was unknown,*
      he found solace under the skies
      and flourished, protected by heaven,
10   until each one of the neighboring peoples
      across the whale-road* yielded tribute.
      That was a good king.
      God had seen the lordless nation
      distressed by a painful absence,
      and so, to console the people, He blessed
      Scyld's dwelling with a young son.
      The Lord of Life granted this son, Beow,*
      worldly honor for his deeds. Beow's prestige
      spread far and wide throughout Scandinavia.
20   Just as Beow did, a young man should practice
      good works through generous treasure-giving
      while under his father's guidance,
      so that in years and wars to come
      dear companions might stand by him.
      A generous man will always prosper.*

      The powerful Scyld departed
      at the fated hour; his soul sought
      the protection of the Lord. His men
      carried his body toward the sea.
30   This he had asked while he could yet wield words,
      the friend of the Scyldings
      who had long ruled the land.
      His icy ship stood at the harbor,

34 "Ring-giver" (*beaga bryttan*) is a common kenning that refers to a king. The exchanging of gifts proves one of the most dominant social practices within Anglo-Saxon society. In exchange for loyal service, the king was expected to reward his warriors and retainers with treasure won in battle. Because these gifts often came in the form of gold rings, which could include bands of gold worn on the finger, or around the neck or arms, "ring-giving" was used metonymously for distributing treasure.

38 The poem does not seem to explicitly recognize a distinct narrator. "I heard" may be a vestige of the oral tradition from which legends like *Beowulf* developed.

45 This is an example of the rhetorical trope called litotes, which appears not infrequently in Old English poetry. Litotes utilizes understatement to emphasize a point. It is used here to highlight Scyld's humble beginnings. Because Scyld was sent over the sea without gifts as a child, the statement that his gifts in death would be greater becomes exceedingly obvious.

51 The line parallels the biblical description of Moses in Deuteronomy 34: "He was buried in a valley in the land of Moab, opposite Beth-peor, but no one knows his burial place to this day."

I. In the manuscript, the poem is divided into forty-three fitts, or sections, with the first fifty-two lines serving as a preface. Most of the fitt divisions are marked with Roman numerals. It is difficult to know whether the fitt divisions reflect the intention of the poem's unknown author or whether they were added by the scribes who copied the poem.

64 The manuscript is unclear here, obscuring information about Healfdane's fourth child, a daughter named Yrse. In some legends, Yrse was not the daughter of Healfdane, but rather both the daughter and wife of Halga (making her Healfdane's daughter-in-law). She ran away to the Swedish king Onelan after her incestuous relationship was revealed. Stories involving incest were common in Germanic legend, but the *Beowulf* poet does not deal explicitly with these themes.

eager to depart. They laid their beloved ring-giver*
beneath the mast, held in the ship's embrace.
Beside him they placed lavish war-treasure,
riches acquired from distant lands.
I have not heard* of a more splendid ship
loaded with weapons and armor,
40   swords and coats of mail.
They laid many treasures on his body
to sail with him into the sea's keeping.
The gifts bestowed upon him in death
were greater than those given to him
as a child,* when he was first sent alone
over the waters. With heavy hearts
they placed a golden flag above his head;
with great mourning they released him
to the sea's care. No hero
50   or wise man can truthfully tell
who under heaven received this cargo.*

I.*
After his father departed from these lands,
Beow of the Scyldings lived among the strongholds,
a dear-loved king of people
and long-standing ruler of nations.
His exalted son, Healfdane, took charge
over the troops. Far into old age,
he was gracious to his people
and fierce in battle. From him
60   four children entered the world,
the good Heorogar and Hrothgar and Halga.
I have heard of a daughter as well
who served as wife and dear bedfellow
to Onela, the Swedish king.*
Hrothgar was granted great success in battle,
such war-glory that friends and kinsmen

69 The mead-hall has many names, such as "wine-hall" and "ring-hall," indicating its many uses. It was a place of assembly, boasting, feasting, distribution of treasure, and entertainment. For Scandinavian and Anglo-Saxon cultures, the mead hall was the center of social life and served as a symbol of social unity.

74 The limits placed on Hrothgar's powers by the phrase *swylc him God sealde, / buton folcscare ond feorum gumena* has been the subject of some debate. Many scholars have understood *folcscare* as referring to "common land," such as open pastures and woodlands that would have been available to members of the community. Stefan Jurasinski argues that *folcscare* refers not to land belonging to the people but rather to the ancestral lands that belong to a royal family. Therefore, Hrothgar is allowed to distribute any goods that come into his possession, but he cannot give away any real estate that he owns by family right and that should be bequeathed to his sons.

87 These lines foreshadow the eventual destruction of Heorot by fire in battle. The Old English poem *Widsith* catalogues the events: war broke out between the Heathobards and the Danes and the battle came to Heorot, where Hrothgar and his nephew Hrothulf together defeated Ingeld of the Heathobards, who was married to Hrothgar's daughter Freawaru. Beowulf himself describes the origins of this conflict in lines 2040-90.

88 Grendel is introduced with the Old English word *ellen-gæst*, a compound noun that can be read a number of ways. The noun *ellen* can mean "bold" or "powerful," while the adjective *ellende* means "foreign, strange," or "exiled." We chose to call Grendel both "powerful" and "an outcast" in order to convey both senses of *ellen-gæst*. We here render *gæst* as "demon" to indicate Grendel's monstrosity. For discussion of *gæst*'s ambiguity, see the note for line 102.

93 A *scop* is a professional court performer who recited poems in the hall, sometimes with musical accompaniment. The *scop* was afforded special status in the community because he served as both an entertainer and a repository for cultural memory. The word *scop* comes from the verb *scieppan*, which developed into modern English "to shape."

99 The *scop*'s song evokes "Cædmon's Hymn," the earliest Old English poem on record.

eagerly followed him, and each young man
in the troop grew ever stronger.
He then envisioned a great mead-hall.*
70 This hall would be celebrated
throughout the ages, and in that place
he would distribute to young and old
all the gifts God had given him
except inherited land and the lives of men.*
I have heard that he commanded
many people throughout the earth
to adorn this dwelling-place. In a short time,
the greatest of all hall-buildings was constructed.
He who built it named it Heorot,
80 Hrothgar, whose words had power far and wide.
He never failed to fulfill his promise:
to distribute treasure and share
precious ornaments at feasts.
The hall towered, lofty and wide-gabled,
still awaiting the hostile flames;
it would not be long before sword-hate would arise
between Hrothgar and his son-in-law.*

A powerful demon, an outcast*
sheltered by the dark, ached
90 upon hearing the daily festivities
carrying on in the boisterous hall
and the clear music of the poet's lyre.
The *scop*,* who knew the story best,
sang of the creation from long ago
and named the Almighty's earthly works:
God established the radiant land and its surrounding seas
and set the sun and moon as gleaming lights for land-dwellers.
He decorated the earth's surface with limbs and leaves
and shaped each and every thing that now moves about.*

101 The Old English reads *feond on helle*. *Feond* developed into modern "fiend," but literally meant "enemy." This phrase links Grendel to Satan, the enemy of God and mankind. (The word "Satan" is a Hebrew noun meaning "adversary.")

102 The Old English here reads *Wæs se grimma gæst Grendel haten*. The word *gæst* can denote either "stranger, guest" or "ghost, spirit." This ambiguity complicates Grendel's image: one definition portrays him as human-like while the other depicts him as supernatural.

     The etymology of the name Grendel is unclear, but scholars have suggested Grendel was derived from verbs meaning "to grind" or "to drown," as well as the nouns for "evil," "storm," or "lake-sand." Others have suggested Grendel is simply a term for a water monster. In "*Beowulf* and the Psychology of Terror," Michael Lapidge suggests that Grendel's inability to be categorized linguistically increases readerly anxiety about his character.

106 Grendel is described here as *wonsælig wer*, which literally means "unblessed man." The poem uses words like *wer* and *guma* ("man") for Grendel, suggesting that he is human-like. We here use the term "half-man" to reflect the poem's language while making clear that Grendel is not fully human. On the language used to describe Grendel's humanity, see Katherine O'Brien O'Keeffe, "*Beowulf*, Lines 702b-836: Transformations and the Limits of the Human."

107 In the Book of Genesis, Cain and Abel are the first sons of Adam and Eve. After Cain kills Abel out of jealousy, God banishes him from his home and makes him "a fugitive and wanderer on the earth."

110 For the Anglo-Saxons, exile was a particularly heinous punishment because society was organized around kinship and political ties. A man sent into exile no longer had a social identity and may be unable to assimilate into another community, leaving him unprotected and companionless. Two Old English poems, *The Wanderer* and *The Seafarer*, describe the difficulties of living in exile. As a descendent of Cain, Grendel is exiled from both God and humanity.

115 The Book of Genesis and the Book of Enoch both describe a race of giants whose wickedness leads to God's wrath and His flooding of the earth. According to early Christian interpretations of Genesis 6:4, the giants are descendants of Cain. In the ancient Hebrew Book of Enoch, this race of giants is begotten by angels and earthly women. These giants eventually turn against men and devour them, provoking God's retribution. For discussion of this pseudo-apocryphal tradition, see Ruth Mellinkoff's two essays on "Cain's Monstrous Progeny in *Beowulf*."

100 So Hrothgar's warriors celebrated daily,
happy until the hell-fiend* imposed his fury.
The grim guest was called Grendel,*
the infamous frontier-haunter who held
the moors and guarded fen and fortress
in what was once home to the giants.
This woeful half-man* had been banished there
after the Maker condemned him as one of Cain's kin;*
the eternal Lord avenged Abel's death.
Cain received no joy from his crime,
110 but instead God exiled* him far from mankind.
From that sin all strange broods emerged.
The monsters springing forth were much like those
who fought with the Lord long ago.
Giants and sprites and sea-monsters
feuded with God until He paid them retribution.*

II.
After night fell, Grendel set out
to attack the illustrious hall of the Ring-Danes,
who had settled in after their night of drinking.
He found the noble troops asleep after their feast,
120 sorrow and misery far from their minds.
Grim and greedy, the unholy creature was ready.
All at once, Grendel, savage and terrible,
seized thirty sleeping men from their resting place
and fled from there, gloating as he returned home
with his prey. At dawn, after the feast,
a clamoring cry was heaved up.
Grendel's deft destruction was revealed.
The famous king, once so great, sat
joyless and drained, gripped by sorrow
130 as they examined the wretched monster's track.
Grendel's fury, hateful and persistent,
was too severe. And so the wait for their enemy

157 In Anglo-Saxon culture, the family of a man who was murdered expected to be compensated monetarily for their loss by the murderer in the form of *wergild* ("man-payment"). The amount of the *wergild* was determined according to the social class of the victim. Because Grendel is not part of Danish society, the Danes can neither offer him money to stay away, nor can they exact payment of the *wergild* in compensation.

162 In order to foster an ominous tone, the poem switches to present tense here to suggest that these roaming spirits remain a problem.

was not long-endured; little time passed
before they met him again. He came
the next night to wreak more havoc,
feeling no remorse for his violence and hostility,
ensnared by his own wickedness.
His deeds were made known
to those who survived, truly told,
140   a clear sign of the hall-watcher's hatred.
All who sought refuge among beds in private chambers
found security in being far from the fiend.
So Grendel ruled against right, one against all,
until the greatest of halls stood empty.

For twelve winters' time,
the lord of the Scyldings shouldered every misery,
the deep sorrows, the grave misfortunes.
Through sad songs and tales,
word of Grendel's bitter feud
150   spread to men and their sons:
how he long fought against Hrothgar,
how he inflicted terror for many years.
Grendel never intended to make peace
with a single Dane, nor to cease
his rampant slaughter, even for payment.
None of the noblemen could dare expect
restitution from those murderous hands.*
Night after night the vicious demon
lurked and haunted the misty moors,
160   becoming the dark death-shadow
of warriors both proven and untried.
Men know not where these roaming spirits wander.*
The enemy of mankind caused much suffering;
time after time the malevolent attacker
performed violent deeds. In the dark of night
he occupied Heorot, the treasure-decked hall,

168 Grendel claims control of Heorot in the evenings, but God prevents him from violating the sacred space of the throne. Grendel's inability to fully enjoy the benefits of the hall is analogous to his exclusion from God's salvation.

174 The poet here claims that by praying to pagan deities, the Danes are, in effect, seeking comfort from "the slayer of souls," or demonic forces, instead of the Christian God.

193 While most of the kingdoms and tribes mentioned in *Beowulf* have historical counterparts, scholars have not reached consensus on the identity of the Geats or where their homeland may have been located. Linguistically, the Old English name *Geatas* corresponds to the Old Norse *Gautar*, the name of a Germanic group that occupied territory in southern Sweden. Because of difficulties with reconciling the details in the poem with historical evidence, it is possible that the Geats may be "no more than a creation of the mythopoetic imagination" (*Klaeber 4*, lxv).

193 A thane is a high-ranking nobleman in Anglo-Saxon and Danish society. While kingdoms would have a number of thanes who depended on and performed service for the king, in our translation, for the sake of clarity, we reserve "thane" to refer specifically to Beowulf.

In "*Beowulf* and the Origins of Civilization," James Earl explains, "Most men in [the poem's Anglo-Saxon] audience, being of the thegnly class, would have identified with Beowulf in the first part of the poem, insofar as he is an utterly exemplary *thegn*. Beowulf serves both Hygelac and Hrothgar faithfully, without any ambition to supplant or even succeed them, and totally without consideration of their conspicuous faults."

Hygelac is the king of the Geats. Fred Robinson proposes several possibilities regarding the meaning of his name. *Hyge* is the word for "mind"; *lac* may mean "strife, turmoil," or it may be an alternative spelling of the Old English *læc*, meaning "lack." Both of these interpretations suggest mental turmoil for Beowulf's king. See Robinson's essay, "The Significance of Names in Old English Literature" in *The Tomb of Beowulf and Other Essays on Old English*.

but he was never allowed to approach the throne
nor its riches, for he knew not God's love.*
Misery befell the lord of the Scyldings;
170 his spirit grieved. The noblemen often met
in council to consider plans, how the brave ones
might best withstand these sudden horrors.
At pagan temples they paid homage to idols
and prayed aloud to the slayer of souls*
that he might relieve the nation of its distress.
Such was the custom of the heathens,
for they have known hell in their heart-thoughts.
They did not know how to praise
the Lord of the Heavens, the Judge of Deeds.
180 Woe unto him who must cast his soul
into the consoling embrace of the fire
in times of great affliction,
for he can expect no redemption.
Blessed be he who after his death-day
seeks peace in the Father's embrace.

III.
During that time of sorrow, Hrothgar,
son of Healfdane, brooded constantly.
The wise hero was helpless
under the weight of such enduring troubles.
190 The strife was too strong, hateful
and long-lasting, that woe that came to men,
the greatest of night-evils.

                          At home
among the Geats,* a thane of Hygelac*
heard of Grendel's exploits.
Noble and mighty, in this life he was
the strongest of men in those days.
He ordered a sturdy ship to be made ready
that he might traverse the swan-road

229 A retainer is one who has pledged his service to a lord.

and speak with the renowned war-king,
200 Hrothgar, who was in need of men.
This thane was beloved to the councilors,
and they found little fault with his expedition.
Reading the omens, they supported
the brave-hearted man. He chose
from among the Geats the boldest
and keenest of warriors. The sea-skilled thane
pointed to the shore, and the chosen fifteen
boarded the ship. The ship was on the waves,
anchored under the cliffs. Ready warriors
210 climbed onto the prow. The currents of the sea
spiraled against the shore. Men carried
splendid armor and treasure to the hull
of the ship. They set out on their voyage
in a well-braced craft, urged by the wind
over the surging sea. The curved-prow ship,
a foamy-necked bird, had advanced far enough
by the next day that the seafarers could spot
gleaming sea-cliffs, high beaches, broad headlands.
The sea had been traversed,
220 the water-course at its end.
From there the Geats went ashore,
secured the vessel, shook their war-garments,
and thanked God that the way across the waves
proved an easy journey. Then from the wall
the watchman of the Scyldings, stationed
to guard the sea-cliffs, saw the shining
war-gear and shields being hauled out.
Determined to know who these men were,
Hrothgar's retainer* rode toward the shore.
230 With mighty hands, he sternly shook his spear
and with formal words inquired:
"What sort of warriors are you, shielded
by mail-coats, who have guided this tall ship

257 Ecgtheow means "sword-servant" or "one devoted to the sword."

across the seaway? For a long time
I have been a border guard, keeping
watch by the sea in the land of the Danes
so that no hostile fleet could do us harm.
Never has a troop so brazenly attempted
to come here, nor did you have
240 any word of leave from our warriors
or agreement from our kinsmen.
Never have I seen a greater warrior
across the earth than this one among you.
This is no mere hall-retainer carrying such weapons.
May such a striking appearance never belie him.
Now I must know your origin
before you go farther hence.
Are you spies intruding into Danish land?
Now, seafaring strangers, quickly
250 make known where you come from,
and clearly state your intentions."

IV.
In response, the leader of the troops
unlocked his word-hoard:
"We are the Geats, Hygelac's men.
My father was well known among the people
as a noble leader of the vanguard.
His name was Ecgtheow.* He saw many winters
before he departed from our lands.
Throughout the wide world,
260 every wise man remembers him fondly.
We come with good intention
to seek your lord, the son of Healfdane,
protector of the people. Give us good counsel.
I expect there to be no secrets between us.
As you know, if what we have heard is truly spoken,
there is an enemy among the Scyldings

279 The line in Old English reads *gescad witan / worda ond worca*, which could be translated either as "know the difference between words and work" or "be able to judge words and work." The former translation suggests that words and work are fundamentally different, while the latter suggests that they work in concert. We have rendered *gescad witan* as "understand" in order to allow for both readings.

292 Boar-images were believed to offer protection to warriors in battle, preventing penetration by sword point. This idea stemmed from ancient belief in the powers of the boar. Sculpted metal in the shape of a boar might be located either atop the crest of the helmet or above the eyebrow piece.

– I do not know what kind –
a reclusive creature in the dark of night
who inflicts terror and unthinkable evil,
270   humiliation and corpse-fall.
I come with a generous heart
to advise the good and wise Hrothgar
how he might defeat this foe and bring about
a different fate, a remedy for his misfortune.
Otherwise, seething sorrow will surge ever after
as long as the greatest of halls stands on its high ground."

Astride his horse, the fearless watchman spoke:
"A keen warrior, one who thinks clearly,
ought to understand both words and work.*
280   I hear that this is a band of soldiers
loyal to Hygelac, the Scandinavian ring-giver.
I will lead the way. Bring your weapons
and armor. I will order my men to guard
your water-tight ship, beached on the shore,
against any trespasser until it safely carries
your well-loved men, those who do good works,
across sea-currents home to Geatland. Fate granting,
they will come through the storm of battle unharmed."

After these words, the Geats followed him.
290   The broad-beamed ship rested in its place,
rocking with the waves, roped and anchored fast.
Golden boar-shaped images* gleamed
on the men's helmets, stained and fire-hardened,
guarding the wearers from harm.
The battle-minded men clamored to the king's court.
They saw the splendid and gold-adorned hall,
celebrated as the greatest under heaven.
Its light shone across the realm.
The gracious escort pointed to the hall,

328 Only men of a certain rank would have been permitted to eat at the same table as the king. Beowulf is indicating their status by introducing them as "table-mates" of the Geatish lord.

329 This is the first time that the poem's hero is named. Beowulf means "bee-wolf," a kenning for "bear."

300   turned his horse and said, "It is time for me to go.
    May the omnipotent Father hold you
    in his favor during this undertaking.
    Now I will return to my post
    to watch for enemies and guard the shore."

    V.
    The ascending stone path guided the men.
    Their polished, hand-linked ring-mail sang
    as they moved toward the hall, fiercely equipped.
    After leaning their broad shields against the wall,
    the sea-weary men sank to the benches,
310   the clang of their armor reverberating.
    Their spears were collected and stood upright,
    a gray ash-wood forest.
    The iron-clad troop was well-armed.
    A proud retainer came from the hall
    to inquire about the warriors' origins:
    "From where have you come
    carrying your plated shields,
    your silver war-gear, and host of lances?
    I am Hrothgar's messenger and officer.
320   I have never seen such a multitude
    of foreign men looking so brave.
    I expect that you seek Hrothgar
    with bold hearts, not because
    you have been exiled from your land,
    but because you wish to perform a noble service."
    From beneath the brim of his helmet
    the powerful Geat replied:
    "We are Hygelac's table-mates.*
    Beowulf is my name.*
330   I wish to speak to the illustrious king,
    if he will grant us an audience."

332 The Vandals were a Germanic tribe that probably originated in northern Sweden, where there is a town called Vendel. Wulfgar may belong to a noble family from that region. While it may seem surprising that a Vandal, rather than a Dane, holds such an important position in Hrothgar's court, *Klaeber 4* points out that "a king of this stature would naturally be attended by high-ranking persons of various origins."

Wulfgar, a warrior of the Vandals,*
famed for his prowess and wisdom, spoke:
"I will announce your arrival to Hrothgar,
the ring-giver, friend of the Danes,
and famous lord of the Scyldings.
I will speak to him on your behalf
and promptly bring you the response
our good lord thinks fit to give."
340   He hurried to find Hrothgar, old and gray,
sitting together with his band of retainers.
Wulfgar boldly strode forth until
he stood before the Danish king;
he knew well the custom of these people.
Wulfgar spoke to his gracious lord:
"A troop of Geats has arrived,
having sailed across the ocean's expanse.
These soldiers call their leader Beowulf.
He is asking, my king, to exchange words.
350   Do not deny this man your answer, kind Hrothgar.
Judging by this troop's war-equipment,
they seem worthy of respect.
Indeed, the leader is strong, that man
who guided his warriors to this place."

VI.
Hrothgar, protector of the Scyldings, spoke:
"I knew Beowulf well when he was a young man;
his father was called Ecgtheow.
Hrethel, king of the Geats, gave him
his only daughter. His brave son
360   now comes here, reviving a friendship.
Seafarers who delivered gifts to the Geats
have told me of Beowulf's courage in battle,
that he has the strength of thirty men in his hand-grip.
Through His grace, Holy God

376 Some Anglo-Saxon helmets included a full face mask. Inspired by Roman war gear, these masks offered protection to both the head and face.

387 Beowulf's first words to Hrothgar adhere to the conventions of the battle-boast, an important type of speech in Anglo-Saxon heroic literature. Boasting serves as a type of public bragging or formal oath a speaker makes to his audience, as the hero pledges in good faith to perform a courageous deed. Boasts may also be directed at another individual, inciting a verbal exchange called "flyting." The Old English poem *The Battle of Maldon* provides another famous example of boasting in Anglo-Saxon literature.

has sent him to us, the Danes,
giving me hope against Grendel's terror.
To reward his daring spirit,
I will offer him treasures. Make haste,
tell them to come see me, give them word
370   that they are welcome guests of the Danes."
Wulfgar addressed the Geats from the doorway:
"My victorious lord has commanded me
to tell you that he knows your noble lineage
and welcomes you as brave-minded guests
from across the sea. Now you may approach Hrothgar,
wearing your battle gear and war-masks,*
but leave your shields and spears behind,
and let discussion determine their use."
Beowulf rose; his powerful warriors followed.
380   Some stayed to guard the weapons
as the brave one had commanded.
The rest marched together under Heorot's roof.
He stood on the hearth, fearless under his helmet.
His chain-mail glistened, sewn by smith's craft.

Beowulf spoke: "Hail to you, Hrothgar!
I am Hygelac's thane and kinsman;
since youth I have garnered much fame.*
News arrived in my country of Grendel's savagery.
Seafarers told me that the greatest of halls
390   now stands empty and useless to every warrior
after evening light hides under the vault of heaven.
The wisest of my men advised me
to visit you, King Hrothgar, for they know
of my renowned strength. They saw for themselves
how I returned bloodstained from battle
where I bound five foes, annihilated
a race of giants, and slew a water-monster
by night on the waves. I have faced great dangers,

431 Weland was a figure of Germanic legend who forged weapons of superior quality. His role can be compared to that of Vulcan in Roman mythology.

432 The Old English reads *Gæð a wyrd swa hio sceal*. *Wyrd* is the Anglo-Saxon concept of fate.

avenged the persecution of the Geats.
400 The enemies were destined for misery;
I destroyed them.
                    And so I shall meet alone
with Grendel, the vicious adversary.
I desire one favor, lord of the Bright-Danes,
protector of the Scyldings, leader of warriors,
noble friend of the people:
now that I have traveled from afar,
I hope that you do not refuse me,
that you permit me and my men to purge Heorot.
I have also learned that the enemy
410 in his rashness cares not for weapons.
In hopes that my liege lord, Hygelac,
will be proud at heart, I will carry
neither my sword nor my broad golden shield,
but instead I will grapple with my enemy,
contending for life in hand-to-hand combat.
Whomever death takes must trust
in the judgment of the Lord.
If Grendel prevails, he will devour the Geats
without hesitation, feed on glorious warriors
420 in the hall of retainers, as he has often done.
You will not need to hide my gruesome face,
for he would have my head decorated
with blood. If death takes me, Grendel
will carry off my mangled corpse
with intent to feast; the lone walker
will ruthlessly stain the moors.
There will be no need to worry about
my body's disposal. If I fall in battle,
send Hygelac the finest of my garments
430 that have protected my breast,
the handiwork of Weland* and heirlooms of Hrethel.
Fate goes as she will, as she must."*

437 Heatholaf probably means "war-remnant" or "battle-legacy." The Wylfings are assumed to be the same group as the Wulfings, who are mentioned in both *Beowulf* and *Widsith*. The Wulfings occupied a region on the southern Baltic coast in northeast Germany.

VII.

Hrothgar, protector of the Scyldings, spoke:
"Beowulf, my friend, you came here
out of kindness to fight for us.
Your father once incited the greatest of feuds
by slaying Heatholaf the Wylfing.*
The Geats refused to harbor him for fear of war.
From there he crossed the rolling waves
440   to visit the Danes, the Honor-Scyldings.
When I first ruled the Danes in early life,
mine was the jewel of kingdoms,
the treasure-house of heroes.
Heorogar, the son of Healfdane
and my elder kinsman, was dead.
He was better than me.
A sorrow weighs on my heart to admit to any man
the shame Grendel has caused me,
polluting Heorot with his hate-thoughts
450   by performing sudden attacks.
He has depleted my hall-troop;
fate sweeps my kinsmen away
with Grendel's horrific destruction.
God's will could easily thwart this rash foe.
Too often, warriors, having drunk from the ale-cup,
vow that they will wait in the hall
to confront Grendel with fierce swordblades.
By morning, this splendid mead-hall
is stained crimson. When the day grows light,
460   the bench boards are soaked with blood,
Heorot drenched in sword-gore.
I have fewer and fewer loyal men;
death has destroyed them.
Now, sit down to this banquet and revel
in the glory of heroes, as your heart desires."
A bench was cleared in the hall

475 Unferth may mean "non-peace" or "un-intelligent," or it may simply be a proper name without symbolic meaning. In lines 1165 and 1456, Unferth is identified as the court's *þyle*, which is usually understood to mean "spokesman." Fred Robinson argues that Unferth's name and title suggest he is the court jester, though this view has not been widely accepted. See Robinson's essay "Personal Names in Medieval Narrative and the Name of Unferth" in *The Tomb of Beowulf and Other Essays on Old English*.

In the *Beowulf* manuscript, his name is written as Hunferth. Although some have recently argued that Hunferth is correct, scholars have long assumed that the "H" is a scribal error. For discussion of this issue, see R.D. Fulk, "Unferth and His Name."

481 Breca means "breaker" or "wave."

496 The Heatho-Ræms were located in what is now southeastern Norway, on the coast of the Norwegian Sea.

for the Geatish troop. There, the stout-hearted men
sat down with Beowulf, boasting of their strength.
A young attendant performed his duties,
470   carrying ornate cups and pouring bright ale.
When the *scop* sang, his clear voice rang
throughout Hrothgar's hall where heroes
and worthy men sat, Danes and Geats together.

VIII.
From his perch at the foot of the Scylding king,
Unferth,* son of Ecglaf, spoke out,
unleashing a battle-boast.
The famous journey of Beowulf,
the bold seafarer, vexed him
because he wished that no one under heaven
480   be more extraordinary than himself.
"Are you the same Beowulf who challenged Breca*
to a competition in the vast sea?
Out of pride, you both tested those waters;
because of brash foolishness,
you risked your lives in the depths.
No man, friend or enemy, could have dissuaded you
from this perilous journey when you dove
into the water. You swam through the current,
your arms navigating the sea-road,
490   your hands darting about rapidly,
gliding through frigid, surging waves.
For seven nights you were the ocean's plaything,
trapped in an unflagging skirmish. In the swell
Breca dominated you; his strength surpassed yours.
When the morning tide carried him
to the shore of the Heatho-Ræms,*
he sought his own dear home,
gracious sanctuary of the Brondiga tribe,
where he guarded subjects, a stronghold, and treasure.

500 Beanstan is the father of Breca and lord of the Brondingas. Little is known about the Brondinga tribe, but it is believed that they inhabited the southern part of the Baltic Penninsula, in either modern day Sweden or Norway.

500　　Breca, son of Beanstan,* faithfully honored
　　　every promise, keeping his formal vow to you.
　　　Though you have always survived the storm of battle,
　　　when you dare to wait the long night for Grendel,
　　　you will face the worst outcome."

　　　Beowulf, son of Ecgtheow, responded in kind:
　　　"Unferth, my friend, you have told us
　　　all about Breca and his expedition,
　　　but you have spoken after drinking too much beer.
　　　I speak the truth when I say my sea-strength
510　　was greater and my path more obstructed
　　　than that of any other man. When we were boys,
　　　we each boasted as any young man would.
　　　We vowed to venture into the ocean,
　　　risking our lives. We kept to our word;
　　　with brave hands we held bare swords
　　　and rowed out to sea, determined
　　　to defend against water-beasts.
　　　Breca could not swim farther or more quickly
　　　on the flood-waves than I could.
520　　We were on the sea together for five nights,
　　　until the waves swept us apart.
　　　The storm's coldest waters welled up,
　　　night darkened, and the battle-grim north wind
　　　betrayed us; the waves were brutal.
　　　The sea-creatures' appetites were aroused.
　　　They advanced, but my strong woven mail-coat,
　　　bright chains linked by hand, was secure
　　　on my chest, protecting me from danger.
　　　A wicked beast dragged me down to the depths.
530　　It held me fast, fixed in its grip.
　　　I struck my fierce opponent
　　　with the edge of my sword;
　　　this victory was granted by fate.

557 Various places have been proposed as the location of the land of the Lapps, but there is little agreement as to whether the poet is referring to land in Norway, Sweden, or Finland.

564 Beowulf here calls attention to an important aspect of Unferth's past. In a culture that condemns kin-slaying it perhaps seems strange that Unferth would not only be allowed in the mead hall, but given a prominent position and be permitted to speak so openly. Critics have proposed various explanations for Unferth's role in the hall and in the poem.

Unferth may have been exiled from his own community and given refuge by the Danes, as Patricia Silber suggests in "Hunferth and the Paths of Exile." We know that Hrothgar has harbored fugitives before, notably Beowulf's father Ecgtheow (see lines 436-40). Geoffrey Hughes argues that Unferth's presence in the hall signifies the underlying corruption in Hrothgar's court. See also Michael Enright, "The Warband Context of the Unferth Episode."

In the storm of battle, I destroyed
that mighty sea-monster with my own hand.

IX.
Ravenous beasts continued to hound me.
I served them the noble sword, as was fitting.
They got no joy from that feast,
the foul creatures who tried to consume me,
540   as they sat down to their banquet
at the bottom of the sea. In the morning
they lay on the shore, put to sleep by my sword,
the coastline littered with their remains.
Never again on the tall sea have those beasts
hindered seafarers' journeys. As light shone
from the east, God's splendid beacon,
the sea subsided so that I might
look to the headlands, the windy walls.
Fate will often save an undoomed man
550   if his courage is mighty. However it happened,
I slew nine sea-monsters with my sword.
I have never heard of a braver night-battle
under heaven's vault or a man with greater troubles
on the sea-currents. Though weary, I survived
this perilous threat to my life. The surging sea
carried me like a ship on the tide
to the shore of the Lapps.* I have never heard
about you competing in such trying contests,
inflicting terror with your blade.
560   Neither you nor Breca have ever performed
such brave exploits with decorated swords during battle
– by no means do I intend to boast –
although you did happen to become the slayer
of your brothers, your close kinsmen.*
For that you will face damnation,
witty as you may be. I speak the truth,

583 In places this far north, the sun appears to rise from the south or southeast rather than due east. The southern sun may also be an expression of God's favor since, as T. M. Pearce has argued, there was a belief that demons and Hell were located in the north.

590 Wealhtheow's name can be translated as "foreign slave" or "foreign captive." *Weal* may signify that she is Welsh or British but the word can also simply mean "foreign." Despite the suggestion of servitude, a person of nobility (she is identified by Beowulf as "daughter of a king" in line 2194) could retain his or her rank even when living outside of his or her native land. Wealhtheow's name indicates that she was likely sent to Hrothgar and the Scyldings to secure a political alliance through marriage, but as Hrothgar's wife she still enjoys a privileged status in the hall.

600 The poet names Wealhtheow's tribe or nation of origin by stating that she is a "woman of the Helmingas" (*ides Helminga*). In *Widsith*, the king of the Wulfings is named Helm, thus making it possible for Wealhtheow to be of Wulfing descent.

Unferth, son of Ecglaf, when I say that Grendel,
your leader's adversary, would have never inflicted
such recurring terrors on Heorot
570   if indeed your spirit were so cunningly fierce
as you claim it to be. Yet the fiend persists,
having realized that he need not fear
the mighty assault of the Victory-Scyldings.
He exacts tribute, he carries out his pleasure,
sparing not one man of the Danish nation.
He butchers and devours,
for he expects no threat from the Spear-Danes,
but soon I shall offer him the strength and valor
of the Geats in battle. Whoever wishes,
580   return courageously to this mead-hall
after tomorrow's morning breaks,
when the sun, clothed in radiance,
shines from the south on the sons of men."*

Then Hrothgar, the giver of treasures,
was content. Gray-haired and battle-famed,
the lord of the Bright-Danes had heard
Beowulf's steadfast resolve; the people's guardian
trusted in him. Then there was cheering
and laughter among the heroes. Joyful words
590   resounded in the hall. Wealhtheow*
stepped forward, Hrothgar's queen,
cloaked in gold. Mindful of court customs,
she welcomed the guests to the hall.
Then the noble woman presented the cup
first to Hrothgar, guardian of the Danes,
and urged him to rejoice in the beer-drinking,
for he was dear to the people.
He partook in the banquet and hall-cup
with pleasure, that glorious king.
600   The woman of the Helmingas* walked

626 Rendered here as "warrior," the word *aglæca* (and its various forms) can be glossed as something like "formidable opponent." In *Beowulf* it is used to refer both to humans and monsters. Because both Grendel and Beowulf are preparing for an attack, we have used the pronoun "he" in line 630 to maintain ambiguity.

among warriors both proven and untried,
offering each of them a drink from her jeweled cup
until the time arrived that she,
the ring-adorned queen, virtuous in heart,
came to Beowulf and offered him the mead.
She paid respect to the man of the Geats.
With wisdom in her words, she thanked God
that her wish had been fulfilled.
She had hoped for a warrior
610   who would relieve their suffering.
Beowulf, the fearless thane, received the cup
from Wealhtheow, and eager for battle, spoke:
"I had a deliberate intention when I set sail
on the waves with my band of men,
either to fully carry out the will of your people
or to fall in battle, caught in the foe's grasp.
I will complete this extraordinary task
or face my final day in Heorot."
The battle-boast greatly pleased Hrothgar's wife.
620   The noble queen, draped in gold,
proceeded to her king and sat.
Then life in the hall was as before,
mighty words were spoken, and the people
were lively and glad until, after a short time,
Hrothgar sought his evening's rest.
He expected that the warrior* would battle
in his high hall. From the time the sun rose
until night darkened all in concealing shadow,
when wan shapes came stalking under the sky,
630   he had been plotting.
                    The company all stood.
Hrothgar turned to Beowulf,
wishing the other man success
and conferring control of the hall:
"Since I first could raise my shield in hand,

636 These lines are significant for two reasons. As David Day has explained, Hrothgar literally bestows the right to "hold" the hall to Beowulf, an act that encapsulates the Germanic system of guardianship law, the way in which people obtained ownership of land and people in this time. Furthermore, this moment is also figuratively significant. The image of power "held" by one's hands as a tangible thing, transferable to another's, will appear again in the text when Beowulf combats Grendel. This reflects the way that hands function as a symbol for power and dominance throughout the poem.

643 The Old English says that Hrothgar *Wealhþeo secan, / cwen to gebeddan*. Dana Oswald points out that *to gebeddan* ("to go to bed") has a similar connotation as the modern use of the phrase. Hrothgar may be seeking Wealhtheow so that they can take their rest, but he may also be looking for sexual intimacy. The fact that he will later emerge from her *bryd-bure* ("bridebower/bedchamber," line 886) suggests the latter. See also Brian McFadden, "Sleeping After the Feast: Deathbeds, Marriage Beds, and the Power Structure of Heorot."

I have never before entrusted Heorot to another.
Now take this great hall and hold it.*
Think of glory, show your courage, stay vigilant.
You will want for nothing
if you pass through this trial with your life."

X.

640   Hrothgar and his guard retreated;
the protector of the Scyldings left the hall.
The king sought out his queen, Wealhtheow,
wishing to take her to bed.* The people knew
that God had appointed a hall-guardian
against Grendel. He served as champion of the Danes,
keeping watch against the monster.
The man of the Geats had faith in his strength
and God's grace. Beowulf gave up
his fine coat of mail, lifted his helmet
650   from his head, handed over his fierce sword,
and commanded his attendant to keep
his war-equipment. Before he settled in,
the fearless man boasted: "I doubt
that Grendel can best me in any contest.
I will slay him, but not with a sword,
as I easily could. He does not have
the skills to wield arms against me,
though he may savagely attack.
Tonight I must abandon my weapons
660   if a weaponless fight is what he seeks.
God in His wisdom holds the outcome in His hands;
the Holy Lord will judge as He deems fit."

Then the battle-brave warrior lay down
and placed his head on a pillow
as his men reclined around him.
No one thought that Beowulf would live

671 Beowulf's people are sometimes referred to as Weather-Geats, Storm-Geats, and Sea-Geats because their territory was located along the coastline. Applying these terms to the Geats reflects their ability to master the sea even in difficult conditions.

692 Throughout this section, the poem uses the word *rinc* ("warrior") to refer to both Grendel and the Geatish soldiers. Like the poet's use of *wer* (line 106), identifying Grendel as a *rinc* creates a similarity between him and his human opponents.

to see home again nor his people
nor the hall where he was raised.
They had heard that death destroyed
670 many Danish men in this wine-hall.
But God, weaving the fate of the Weather-Geats,*
would give him success in combat.
They would overcome their foe
with the aid of one man. Truly, it is clear
that God has always ruled His people.
That night, under the cover of darkness,
the hell-walker came to hunt.
When they ought to be guarding the gabled hall,
the warriors slept, except for one.
680 The men well knew that while the Lord forbade it,
the demon could not pull them down into shadow.
Beowulf waited awake for the creature,
impatient and filled with battle-rage.

XI.

Then the godforsaken Grendel came
from the moor below the misty slopes.
This scourge of men intended to snatch
Heorot's people. Raging at the heavens,
he stole toward the famed and luminous hall.
This was not the first time Grendel had hunted
690 at Heorot, but never in all his days
would he find harder luck or troops.
The joyless warrior* approached;
the iron-banded door sprang open at his touch.
Enraged, he stood at the mouth of Heorot,
then swaggered across the burnished floor,
his eyes like eerie flames. He saw
many warriors in the hall, the assembled troop
of kinsmen sleeping.
           From anger came laughter.

708 We adopt Fred Robinson's suggestion that *synsnædum* should be read as "sinful morsels." Robinson explains that the word, which appears only in *Beowulf*, invokes cultural anxiety about cannibalism and blood-drinking. He points out, "In Anglo-Saxon times the mention of blood-drinking would probably have suggested a specific and horrifying sin, a sin which would match on a spiritual, theological level the physical horror of Grendel's feast." See Robinson's essay "Lexicography and Literary Criticism: A Caveat" in *The Tomb of Beowulf and Other Essays on Old English*.

The fearsome demon vowed that before daybreak
700   he would rip life from each man's body
      and feed. But after that night, fate would
      no longer allow him to consume that race
      of men. Hygelac's mighty thane watched
      to see how the attack would unfold.
      The deadly foe did not delay.
      He burst in to seize the nearest sleeping man.
      He tore apart his bone-locks, gulped blood
      and swallowed each sinful morsel* until
      he had all but devoured the entire corpse
710   from hands to feet. Next, he stalked
      toward Beowulf's resting place
      and reached for him, but with vicious intent
      the strong-hearted thane resisted his enemy.
      He met Grendel's palm with his own.
      The wicked warrior instantly knew
      that he had never encountered in this world,
      in all the regions of the earth,
      a stronger hand-grip from any other man.
      He felt fear in his heart
720   yet could not break away.
      He thought desperately of escape;
      he wished to flee to his hiding place,
      to return to the clamor of devils.
      Even in days of old he had never faced
      such a challenge. Beowulf remembered
      his evening boast. He stood up
      and grasped firmly, fingers bursting.
      The brute struggled to break loose;
      the nobleman stepped forward.
730   Grendel desired to escape far away
      to his home in the fens. He sensed the power
      in Beowulf's fingers from that hostile grip.
      That was the most grievous journey

736 *Denum eallum wearð…ealuscerwen* can be literally translated as "to all the Danes it was an ale-shower" or, alternatively, "an ale-deprival." *Ealuscerwen* is the most debated word in *Beowulf,* and various interpretations of this line have been proposed over the years. Some critics have suggested that this may be an idiomatic expression that refers to misfortune or some type of calamity. In this context, the "ale-shower" may signify the violence and destruction taking place in Heorot, which the Danes can hear from their own homes.

749 *Klaeber 4* notes that the poet's use of *banfag* ("bone-decorated") could possibly refer to antlers mounted on the wall, or, more likely, to ivory taken from walrus tusks or whale teeth, which would have been carved into expensive ornaments. Perhaps the poet intends a rather dark pun with *banfag* since Heorot has, for the past twelve years, been decorated with the bones of the men who Grendel had killed.

751 In 2013 archaeologists announced that they had uncovered the remains of a hall that may have served as the basis for Heorot in the Danish town of Lejre. Found among the remains were objects that would have been used in feasts, gold jewelry, pottery, and the jawbone of a bear that may have been given as a gift. These artifacts indicate the presence of royalty and the magnificence of the hall.

the guilty ravager ever took to Heorot.
The hall cried out.
Terror arose in all the Danes,*
in every brave subject and nobleman.
Both fierce hall guardians were enraged.
Now the hall bellowed. It was a wonder
740   that the building withstood the great battlers,
that the beautiful wine-hall did not crumble
to the surface of the earth. It was steadfast
inside and out, braced with iron bands
skillfully forged by the smith's hands.
I have heard there were many gold-trimmed
hall benches torn loose from the floor
where the menacing fight occurred.
Until then, the Scylding elders did not think
that the hall, magnificent and ivory-adorned,*
750   could be destroyed by man's scheming
unless embraced in flames, swallowed by fire.*
Startling sounds ascended in waves; terrible fear
rose within the Danes as each of them
heard wailing through the walls. God's foe
sang a song of pain, the hell-captive
lamented his defeat. He held Grendel fast,
he who was the strongest man in those days.

XII.
Beowulf, protector of men, in no way wished
to release the murderous visitor alive,
760   nor did he consider Grendel's life
to be of any value. One after another,
his warriors drew their battle-tested swords,
desiring to protect the life of their lord,
their illustrious prince, as best they could.
When they rushed into combat,
those who sought to pierce the soul

772 The word *ellor-gæst*, here translated as "outcast demon," is used to refer to both Grendel and his mother (at lines 1344, 1626, and 1630). *Ellor* means "other" or "foreign," and the repeated use of this term has led some scholars to believe that the previous identification of Grendel as *ellen-gæst* (discussed in the note for line 88) is a scribal error for the more usual *ellor-gæst*.

of the sinful scourge did not know
that the best war-sword's iron on earth
could never harm him. His curse
770   had made each victory blade useless.
On that day, the last of his life,
the outcast demon* was meant to die
a wretched death and journey deep
into the realm of fiends. He who had injured
the hearts of men through outrageous violence,
he who feuded with God, discovered
that his body would no longer endure.
The courageous thane of Hygelac
held fast to Grendel's hand.
780   While both lived, they existed in hatred.
The terrible foe felt bodily pain
as a fatal wound split his shoulder.
Sinews sprang apart and bone-locks burst.
Triumph in battle was granted to Beowulf.
Grendel, mortally wounded, fled
under the fen-slopes to his joyless dwelling;
he knew his days had come to an end.
After the deadly encounter, the wish of the Danes
was realized. The strong and wise man
790   cleansed the hall. He who had come from afar
saved the Danish king from affliction.
The Geatish man rejoiced in his deed of valor.
He had fulfilled his boast to the Danes.
He remedied the desperate sorrow
that once had plagued them;
out of dire necessity they had become
accustomed to profound suffering.
Afterwards, the brave man fastened
Grendel's entire claw, his arm
800   and shoulder together, under the high roof.
That was a clear sign.

XIII.

As I have heard, when morning came
many a warrior gathered in the gift-hall.
Powerful men from near and far,
from distant regions, traveled to examine
this wondrous thing, the hated foe's tracks.
His departure did not cause grief
to any man who saw how Grendel fled,
who examined the footprints of the vanquished.
810   He had been defeated, heart-weary
and doomed, and had taken his mortal steps
into the water-monsters' marsh.
There the bloody waters surged,
terrible swirls seethed, the waves
stirring up hot blood and sword-gore.
Death-doomed and joy-deprived,
Grendel hid in the refuge of the fen
and laid down his life, his heathen soul.
Hell received him there.
820   On horseback, spirited and happy,
old and young warriors rode back from the lake.
Beowulf's glorious deed was proclaimed.
It was widely declared that no other shield-warrior,
north or south, between the two seas,
across the vast earth, under the sky,
could be better or more worthy.
However, they did not place any blame
on gracious Hrothgar, their lord and friend,
for that was a good king.
830   The battle-brave men felt free
to race their tawny horses, galloping
where the familiar path seemed smooth
and pleasant. At times the king's retainer,
a man gifted in reciting song, recounted
many ancient sagas, finding new words

840 The *scop* delivers a story based on the Norse legend of Sigemund, which came to be presented in the thirteenth-century Old Icelandic *Volsunga Saga*. Sigemund is a solitary warrior who, like Beowulf, performs many heroic tasks in fighting against enemies both human and supernatural. Here, the *scop* refers to Fitela (a version of the Old Norse name Sinfjötli) as Sigemund's *nefa*, which was an Old English word that could refer to either an illegitimate son or a nephew. In some accounts of the legend Fitela is both, having been born after Sigemund was tricked into an incestuous encounter with his sister, Signý. In the *Volsunga Saga* and other Norse and Germanic accounts, it was not Sigemund but rather his son, Sigurðr, who famously slew a dragon. It is unclear whether there was an earlier Scandinavian version that attributes the dragon-slaying to Sigemund as the *scop* does here. For discussion of parallels between Sigemund and Beowulf, and the problematic nature of the comparison, see Mark S. Griffith, "Some Difficulties in *Beowulf*, lines 874-902: Sigemund Reconsidered."

864 Heremod (literally "battle-hearted/spirited" or "war-minded") was a legendary Danish king who serves here as a foil to both Sigemund and Beowulf. While Sigemund flourishes because of his consistent strength and courage, the once-great Heremod fails as a leader. Critics have suggested that Heremod may be based on account of the Danish king Lother in Book 1 of Saxo Grammaticus' *Gesta Danorum*. Lother usurps the throne from his brother, rules as a tyrant, and is then killed in a popular uprising against his wicked rule.

868 The similarity between the Old English words *eoten* and *Eotan* presents textual and interpretive problems. The former means "giants," while the latter refers to the Jutes, a Germanic tribe that occupied parts of what is now Denmark and who settled in England in the sixth century. In certain places where the poem uses a form of *eoten*, the context has suggested to some scholars that *Eotan* would be more fitting, and they have regarded *eoten* as a scribal error. That is, some think the scribe wrote "giants" when he really meant "Jutes." At other places in the poem, context suggests that *eoten* most likely refers to "giants," such as line 114, which discusses God's feud with "giants and sprites and sea-monsters."

The *eoten/Eotan* issue stems from the poem's mixture of history and mythology. In the poem's allusion to Heremod (lines 861-879) and in the Finn episode (lines 1037-1140), narratives that seem to concern conflicts between men, perhaps with a basis in actual events, the presence of Jutes would be more expected than the presence of giants. As a consequence, a majority of scholars subscribe to this view. Alternatively, John Vickrey believes that these episodes have roots in folklore, and so he argues that the poet is referring to giants instead of Jutes.

Rather than reading *eoten/Eotan* literally, Robert Kaske has suggested that the poet uses *eoten* ("giant") as an epithet. We agree with Kaske that the poet's use of *eoten* in these instances is a means of negatively characterizing the

and masterfully joining them. The man
took on the task of narrating Beowulf's feat,
elegantly crafting the tale, weaving his words.
He then fashioned a song from what he had heard
840   of Sigemund's deeds of courage,*
many of them previously unsung,
his struggles, his distant conquests,
feuds and violence that no one had heard before,
except for Fitela. When Sigemund wished
to divulge his battle stories to him,
uncle to nephew, Fitela was always there.
Close comrades in battle, they eliminated
whole races of giants with their swords.
Sigemund's legacy flourished after his death-day.
850   Hardened by war, he boldly slew a dragon,
a hoarder of treasure. This nobleman's son
had ventured without Fitela, alone
on a daring exploit into the gray stone cave.
His noble iron sword impaled the awful dragon
and fixed him to the wall, a violent and fatal assault.
The combatant's courage had allowed him
to control the ring-hoard at his own discretion.
Sigemund, son of Wæls, loaded his ship
with bright treasures that he had obtained.
860   The fire-dragon was consumed by its own flame.
Sigemund was a hero across nations,
renowned far and wide as a protector
of warriors because of his brave deeds.
He thrived after Heremod's rule.*
King Heremod had been strong and courageous,
but his battle prowess diminished.
He was led astray into the control of his enemies,
those brutes,* and was soon murdered.
His sorrow-surge had crippled him
870   for too long. He became a threat

enemies of the Danes. The poet, in our opinion, uses "giant" much in the same way a modern speaker might refer to another person as a "monster." Therefore, where the poet uses forms of *eoten* or the phrase *bearn eotena* ("sons of giants") when referring to enemies of the Danes, we use "brutes." This conveys the pejorative sense while maintaining the humanity of the subjects.

to his subjects and noblemen. Wise men
longingly remembered the earlier times,
when the stout-hearted one had success.
They had trusted in his remedy for evil,
certain that the son of the king would prosper,
inherit his father's virtue, protect the people,
their treasure, his lordly home, the hero's
kingdom, and the native land of the Scyldings.
Instead, he was imbued with wickedness.
880   Beowulf, however, was cherished by friends and kin.
Soon the morning light pushed at the horizon.
The warriors on horseback still traversed
the dusky road. Many of them went
to the high hall to see the strange wonder.
The king himself, that ring-guardian,
came from the queen's bedchamber.
Nobly esteemed, flanked by his troops,
alongside his queen and her ladies,
he advanced to the mead-hall.

XIV.
890   Hrothgar approached the hall.
He stood on the steps, gazing at the lofty roof
adorned with gold and Grendel's hand
and said: "May thanks now be given to God
for this token. I anticipated many more
of Grendel's hateful visits,
but God, the guardian of glory,
always delivers wonder after wonder.
It was not long ago that I had stopped expecting
to see any relief from this misery;
900   my best house stood blood-spattered and defiled.
The wise men, shaken by despair,
did not know how to defend the land
from such evil, demons and deadly spirits.

909 Hrothgar had implied that Beowulf's mother was the daughter of Hrethel at line 358, but here he seems not to know anything about her.

911 Hrothgar's statement to Beowulf, "*me for sunu wylle / freogan on ferhþe*," is ambiguous enough to be problematic. The Danish king may be stating his intention to formally adopt Beowulf as his own son or he might simply be expressing affection for the Geatish hero. Wealhtheow will later address this ambiguity and ask Hrothgar to respect the inheritance rights of his children.

926 The Old English phrase *feond on frætewum* ("the enemy in his armor") would have typically been used to describe human warriors, but it is here used figuratively since Grendel does not wear actual armor. The *frætewum* could refer to Grendel's skin, or the phrase may be used here to again blur the distinction between Grendel as man and Grendel as monster.

Now, through the power of the Lord,
a thane has deftly performed a deed
that we never could. Whichever woman
gave birth to this man, if she still lives,
can say that the everlasting God was gracious
in bringing her son into the race of men.*
910 *Hwæt*, Beowulf, finest of men,
in my heart I will love you as a son.*
Tend to this new relationship,
and you will lack nothing in this world
that I have the power to provide.
Often I have rewarded lesser men for lesser deeds,
given gifts to those inferior to you in battle.
You yourself have accomplished such a feat
that your glory will live on forever.
God will repay you with goodness,
920 as He has always done."

Beowulf, son of Ecgtheow, spoke:
"With good will, we have fought,
performed courageous deeds,
and dared to face the power of the unknown.
Indeed, I wish that you had been able
to see the fiend fallen in his armor.*
I quickly decided to grasp him
and bind him to his deathbed.
In my hand-grip he would writhe
930 in fatal torment, unless he could break free.
But I could not hinder his escape,
for God did not will it,
though I firmly held the deadly foe.
The enemy was too powerful in flight,
yet he lost his hand trying to keep his life.
His arm and shoulder remain behind.
The wretched half-man could not buy any relief.

956 There is a kind of joke in the poet's use of the phrase *folmum gefrætwod*, which can be translated as "decorated by hands" or "decorated with hands." While the literal meaning is that people should adorn the hall with ornaments, Heorot is also "hand-decorated" now that Grendel's severed arm hangs on the wall.

Surely that bringer of evil will not live long,
tormented by his own wrongdoing.
940 His pain wraps him tightly in a cruel grip,
baleful bonds; now he must wait,
outlawed by his wickedness,
until glorious God passes his judgment."
Unferth, son of Ecglaf, was silent,
his battle-boasting halted
as every nobleman beheld the hand
hanging under the high roof,
proof of the thane's craft.
At the tip of the fiend's fingers
950 were nails like steel, the warrior's
heathen hand-spurs, hideous and awful.
It was said that no trusted sword
could harm the enemy, no weapon
could weaken his bloodstained battle-hand.

XV.
Soon it was commanded that
Heorot's interior be hand-decorated.*
There were many people, men and women,
who dressed the guest-hall. Gold-trimmed tapestries
shone on the walls, wondrous sights
960 to those who gazed upon them.
Splendid as it was, the greatest of halls
was shattered; all throughout the interior
the firm iron hinges had sprung apart.
The roof alone survived, sound in every regard
after the sin-stained creature turned in flight,
despairing for his life. Try as one might,
it is not easy to flee from death:
all soul-bearers, children of men,
people of the earth, must seek their resting place,
970 the bed of death where the body lies,

978 Hrothulf is the son of Halga, Hrothgar's younger brother. Hrothgar and Wealhtheow adopted Hrothulf after the untimely death of his parents.

983 The treachery alluded to may be the eventual murder of Hrethric, Hrothgar's son, by Hrothulf so that he can usurp the throne. According to some versions of Danish history and legend, Hrothulf is depicted as ambitious and brutal, and his actions eventually lead to the decline of the Scyldings. Other Scandinavian literature casts Hrothulf in a more favorable light, making no mention of a violent usurpation, and so this reference remains ambiguous.

990 This is probably another example of litotes, as Beowulf would have been proud to receive these gifts, particularly in a culture where a warrior expected rewards for exceptional performance.

996 Some Anglo-Saxon helmets included an iron ridge that ran from the forehead to the nape of the neck which provided a small degree of extra protection. The gold wires were most likely decorative.

held fast in sleep after feasting.

Then it was the time and occasion
for Hrothgar to return to the hall;
he wished to partake in the banquet.
I have never heard of a greater company,
a people who conduct themselves better
when gathered around their treasure-giver.
The glorious leaders, Hrothgar and Hrothulf,*
sat down on the bench and rejoiced at their feast.
980 Their kinsmen courteously passed around
many cups of mead in the illustrious hall.
Heorot was filled with friends;
no treachery did the Scyldings yet perform.*
Then Hrothgar gave his father's sword
to Beowulf and rewarded him with a golden
banner of victory, a helmet, and mail-coat.
Many a renowned man watched
as the fine sword was brought before the warrior.
Beowulf drank from a cup;
990 he had no need to feel shame* for receiving
such rewards in the presence of other warriors.
I have heard of few men who have given
such treasures in a friendlier manner,
four gifts adorned in gold.
A ridge wound with wires ran across the top
of the helmet from front to back,*
guarding him so that battle-hardened swords
do not gravely injure the shield-bearer
when he must march against enemies.
1000 Hrothgar commanded eight horses
with gold-plated bridles to be led inside the hall.
One horse stood alone wearing a saddle
skillfully decorated with shining precious jewels.
That had been the war seat of the high king

1020 Hrothgar generously offers to pay the *wergild* that Grendel owes for killing Beowulf's companion (lines 706-10).

1036 The *scop* begins to recount a story known as the Finn Episode. Finn's men, the Frisians, were a Germanic people who occupied land along the coast of the Netherlands, northwestern Germany, and Denmark. The Old Frisian language was closely related to Old English. Parts of this story, which would have been familiar to an Anglo-Saxon audience, are made known to us in *Beowulf* and in another Old English poem, of which only 47 lines remain extant, known as *The Finnsburh Fragment.*

     The story is as follows: The Danish leader Hnæf and a group of his warriors take shelter with King Finn of the Frisians during the winter. The Danes are guests in Finn's mead-hall when they are attacked by Finn's men. Hnæf is killed and Hengest becomes the leader of the Danes. Over the course of a few days, a battle is fought in which the Danes are able to hold the hall but unable to fight their way out, while the Frisians, having lost a great number of men, are unable to defeat the Danes. Eventually, a call for peace is made, and the Danes agree to accept Finn as their new lord until the winter passes and they can make their way home. The Danes pledge to serve Finn and, in return, Finn agrees to treat the Danes as his own retainers. When spring arrives, the Danes travel across the sea and prepare to avenge the wrongs committed by the Frisians. A Danish army returns to Frisia, defeats Finn and his warriors, and recovers Hildeburh, the Danish sister of Hnæf who had been married to Finn as a peace-pledge.

whenever he wielded his sword in battle.
At the head of the vanguard, Hrothgar's courage
never failed when the corpses fell.
Then the lord of the Danes granted ownership
of horses and weapons to Beowulf
1010 and ordered him to make good use of them.
Thus the illustrious king, the treasure-keeper,
repaid the hero for his bravery in battle
with horses and gifts of such quality
that man will never find fault with them,
as one who speaks the truth will relay.

XVI.
Hrothgar also gave treasured heirlooms
to each warrior on the mead-bench
who had undertaken the sea-journey with Beowulf,
and he ordered that the Geats be repaid with gold
1020 for Grendel's murder of their comrade.*
There would have been more deaths
had not wise God and the courage of one man
prevented that fate. God ruled over all
the race of men, as He does to this day.
Therefore, it is best to be understanding
in every respect and be mindful of the future.
He who lives long in these days of strife
shall know much love and loathing.
Then, song and music were presented
1030 before Hrothgar, the Danish battle-leader.
The harp was strummed and tales recounted
as Hrothgar's *scop* told of Finn's men,
performing among the mead-benches.
A sudden attack befell the heroes
of the Half-Danes; Hnæf of the Scyldings
had to fall in the Frisian onslaught.*

1039 The poem uses the word *eotena* to refer to the Frisians here, at line 1059, and at 1120. On the word *eotena* and our use of "brutes," see note for line 868.

1054 Hengest becomes the leader of the Danish troop after Hnæf is killed. According to Bede's *Ecclesiastical History of the English Speaking People*, one of the two Germanic chieftains who led the settlement of England in the fifth century was named Hengest. Whether the Hengest mentioned here is meant to refer to the historical Hengest is unclear.

1055 The Old English is ambiguous as to who offered terms to whom.

Indeed, Hildeburh, royal sister of Hnæf,
had no reason to praise the good faith
of those brutes.* Though guiltless,
1040   she was deprived of her dear ones,
sons and brothers fallen to their fate
in shield-play, wounded by spears.
That was a sad woman.
This daughter of Hoc had cause
to mourn at morning's light,
when she could see their destined end,
the slaughter of her kinsmen,
under the sky where she once held
the greatest joy in the world.
1050   The fight had destroyed all of Finn's retainers
except a lone few, so he could not
fight to the finish in that meeting-place
nor force out the Danish survivors
and Hengest,* Hnæf's thane.
So terms were offered:*
The Frisians would provide floor space,
clear the hall and throne,
so that the Danes might be allowed
to share control of the hall with those brutes.
1060   Also, on each day of treasure-gifting,
Finn, the son of Folcwadan, would honor
the Danes, presenting Hengest's troop
with rings just as graciously as he honors
the Frisians with gold-plated treasure
in this beer-hall. Then both sides pledged
an unyielding peace treaty.
With sincere courage Finn swore to Hengest,
according to the judgment of his council,
that he would hold with honor
1070   the Danish survivors of that slaughter.
It was sworn that no man would break

1088 The poem uses litotes here: *sume on wæle crungon* ("some had fallen in battle").

this treaty through words or deeds,
nor with malice should the Danes
ever complain, even though,
having lost a lord, they were forced to follow
the man who murdered their ring-giver.
If any Frisian spoke of that deadly hatred
and stirred the Danes' memory,
he would have to face the sword's edge.
1080 The funeral pyre was prepared,
and mighty gold spilled from the hoard.
The best of the Scylding warriors
was ready to be laid on the pyre.
His golden, bloodstained mail-coat
with iron-forged boar images
was easily seen among the warriors
who died from their wounds.
Many had fallen in battle.*
Hildeburh commanded that her own son
1090 be committed to the fire next to Hnæf,
that the bone-vessel be placed
on the pyre at his uncle's shoulder.
The woman lamented with a song of mourning.
The warrior was lifted.
The greatest of funeral fires spiraled
to the clouds, roaring above the barrow,
heads consumed by flames.
Gashes burst open and blood
streamed forth from the body's scars.
1100 The flame, greediest of ghosts,
swallowed all those who had fallen
there in war, men of both nations.
Their glory had passed away.

1120 We agree with Scott Gwara, who argues in *Heroic Identity in the World of Beowulf* that the poet's use of *gemunde* (past tense form of "to remember") is best understood as a euphemism for "give compensation" or "take revenge" (pp. 171-2). In modern English, "repay" can communicate both senses.

1121 In honoring the code of vengeance, Hengest must violate his truce with Finn.

1122 Hunlafing means "son of Hunlaf." He appears to be a Danish leader, although little else is known about his identity. Chickering suggests "Hunlaf was probably a brother of Guthlaf and Oslaf who fell at Finnsburh, since [Old Norse] forms of their three names appear together in a list of Danish princes in the *Skjøldunga saga*" (p. 327). Some critics have suggested that Hunlafing is actually the name of the sword rather than the man who gives a sword to Hengest.

XVII.
Deprived of friends, the warriors
departed for Frisia, seeking their homes.
Having no other options, Hengest remained
with Finn throughout the slaughter-stained winter.
He longed for his home, but he could not
sail over the waters on a curved-prow ship.
1110 The sea surged with storms, water fought
against wind, winter locked the waves
with an icy bond until the other season came,
spring to the homes, as it always does.
Glory-bright weather always obeys its season.
Winter had passed. The earth's bosom grew fair.
The exile became restless; the guest
departed from that land. He thought
more of revenge than the sea-voyage,
whether he should wage war
1120 to repay* those brutes. Thus Hengest
did not break the code of vengeance*
when Hunlafing* placed on his lap
the gleaming battle-sword whose blade
was known among the Frisians.
In turn, cruel death by the sword
befell bold-hearted Finn at his own home
when Guthlaf and Oslaf, bemoaning
their sorrows after their sea-voyage,
assigned him blame for their share of misery.
1130 The enraged heart could not restrain itself.
The hall was reddened with the blood of their enemies.
In this attack Finn was slain, the king
among his warrior troop, and his queen
reclaimed. The Scylding archers
carried to the ship the king's goods,
the jewels and precious gems,
all that they had found.

1149 On the character of Hrothulf and the possibility of treachery, see note for line 983.

They carried the noble woman
on the sea-journey to the Danes,
1140 led her back to her people.

The song was sung to its end,
the tale of the musician. Merriment arose
once more, the hall-noise sounding clearly.
Cup bearers gave wine from handsome vessels.
Crowned in gold, Wealhtheow came forth
and approached the two good men,
uncle and nephew, Hrothgar and Hrothulf.
Their peace was still secure, each one
loyal to the other.* Unferth,
1150 the court spokesman, sat at the feet
of the Scylding king. Everyone trusted
in Unferth's bold spirit, though he was not
kind to his kinsmen when swordblades clashed.
Then the Scylding queen spoke:
"Receive this cup, my noble lord and ring-giver.
Be glad, gold-friend to men, and speak
generous words to the Geats, as a man must.
Be gracious with them, and be mindful
of the gifts from far and near that you now hold.
1160 I have heard that you wish to have
this warrior, Beowulf, as a son.
Heorot, the shining hall, has been cleansed.
Enjoy the many rewards as long as you may,
but leave the troop and kingdom to your kinsmen
when you go forth to your destined end.
I have faith in my gracious Hrothulf.
He plans to rule the young warriors with kindness
should you depart this world before him.
If he remembers all that we did when he was a child
1170 to fulfill his desires and establish his worldly name,
I expect that he, through good deeds,

1173 Hrethric means "famous ruler." Hrothmund means "famous hand."

1185 The necklace Wealhtheow gives to Beowulf is compared to the *Brosinga mene* (Brosings' necklace), which, in Norse mythology, is a valued treasure that Loki stole from the goddess Freyja. The poem here implies that the *Brosinga mene* eventually came to be owned by Eormenric and was then stolen by Hama, an allusion to the conflict between Erminríkr and Heimir that is part of the Norse saga tradition. The story is recounted in the thirteenth-century *Thidreks Saga*. For discussion of the legendary necklace's significance, see Tomoaki Mizuno's "The Magical Necklace and the Fatal Corslet in *Beowulf.*"

1188 In *Thidreks Saga*, Heimir enters a monastery after fleeing from Erminríkr. As Chickering explains, "At the very least, to 'choose eternal reward' is to become Christian and also, in this context, to give up worldly goods. It may also be a periphrasis for 'to die'" (p. 332).

1190 The neck-ring referred to here is the one that Wealhtheow is giving to Beowulf. The poet is jumping ahead in time to explain that this neck-ring will eventually be lost when Beowulf's king, Hygelac, wears it into battle during his disastrous raid against the Frisians. The abrupt leap in chronology helps establish the contrast between Hama and Hygelac. As Robert Kaske points out in "The Sigemund-Heremod and Hama-Hygelac Passages in *Beowulf*," Hama had carried the *Brosinga mene* out of danger to a safe place, but Hygelac took his necklace from a safe place and carried it into danger. Hygelac's assault on the Frisians will be referred to throughout the last third of *Beowulf*.

will repay our sons." She went to the bench
where her boys, Hrethric and Hrothmund,*
sat together with young warriors and sons of heroes.
There, too, Beowulf, good man of the Geats,
sat beside the two brothers.

XVIII.
A cup was brought to him
and friendly invitation offered.
Twisted bands of gold were kindly bestowed:
1180   two arm-bands, a coat of mail, rings,
and what I have heard to be
the greatest neck-ring on earth.
No better treasure under the sky
has been heard of since Hama carried off
the necklace forged by the Brosings,*
jewel and precious setting, to the shining stronghold.
He fled the wrath of Eormenric
and chose eternal benefits.*
Hygelac of the Geats, nephew of Swerting,
1190   wore this neck-ring* in his final battle
while he guarded the spoils of war,
defended his treasure beneath the banner.
Fate brought him to destruction when,
out of pride, he sparked a feud with the Frisians,
bringing misery and hostility upon himself.
This mighty king wore his treasure-garments
and precious stones across the ocean.
He then fell beneath his shield in battle.
The body of the king passed
1120   into the possession of the Franks,
along with his breast-plate
and that jeweled necklace.
Lesser warriors pillaged the slain
after the battle-carnage. Geatish men

littered the bone-yard.
                              The hall echoed with sound.
Wealhtheow spoke to all assembled:
"Enjoy this ring, beloved Beowulf,
fortunate young man. Make use of this garment
and the people's treasures, and prosper.
1210   Gain fame through valor, and to my sons
be gracious in giving counsel.
I will remember such kindness.
You have made it so that far and near,
forever and always, men will esteem you.
Your fame is wide as the walled sea,
the home of the winds. May you live well
as a favored prince. I wish for you great treasure.
Be good to my sons, joyous one.
Here each loyal warrior is true to one another
1220   and obliging to his generous lord;
the retainers are a fully-prepared, united people.
Having drunk from the cup, the men do as I ask."
The queen then returned to her seat,
and the best of banquets took place: the men drank.
They did not know the grim fate
that would come to the warriors when evening fell.
Hrothgar departed to his bedchamber,
the mighty one to his resting place.
Countless warriors occupied the hall,
1230   as they often had before. The benches
were cleared and covered with bedding and pillows.
One of these beer-drinkers, ill-fated
and about to die, lay down to slumber.
The men set bright wooden shields
close by. Each warrior's tall helmet,
ring-mail corslet, and mighty spear
were readily seen on the benches above him.
It was their custom to be ready for war,

1244 This is an ironic reference to the twelve years that Hrothgar and the Danes had abandoned Heorot in the evenings so that they might avoid Grendel's attacks.

1250 The term *aglæcwif*, which is used to refer to Grendel's mother, combines an ambiguous term for a monster or a formidable opponent (*aglæc*) with the term for woman (*wif*). As Melinda Menzer has shown, Old English *wif* "always refers to a woman, rather than a female being," and so the term casts Grendel's mother as a person and not simply a beast. In our translation, we have separated the compound and tried to give equal weight to her monstrosity and her humanity. See the note for line 626 on Grendel and Beowulf as *aglæca*.

1266 The poem here calls Grendel a *helle-gæst*. As noted in line 88, *gæst* can mean either "guest" or "ghost, demon." Additonally, *helle* might refer to either its cognate, "hell," or, alternatively, "hall." Therefore this word can be read both as "hell-demon" and "hall-guest."

both at home and in battle, at any such occasion
1240 that the need of their liege lord arose.
That was a good people.

XIX.
                            They sank to sleep.
Someone paid dearly for his evening's rest,
as had often happened to them since
Grendel had become guardian of the golden hall,*
worked his evil until his end came,
death the penalty for his wrongdoing.
It became evident, widely known among men
that an ancient avenger yet lived
in grief-laden torment after the creature's fall.
1250 Grendel's mother, both woman and monster,*
languished in misery, condemned to live
in the awful water, the cold marsh,
since Cain had become the slayer
of his only brother, his father's son.
Guilty and marked with murder,
he departed, fled the pleasures of human life
to dwell in the wasteland. From him sprang forth
many doomed creatures; one was Grendel,
the seething outcast, who found the man at Heorot
1260 awake and waiting for his fight.
There his adversary grasped him.
Beowulf remembered his strength,
the great gift given to him by God,
and he depended on grace from the Ruler,
solace and support. With these gifts,
he overcame his enemy, humbled the hell-demon.*
The wretched one departed to seek
his death-bed, robbed of all gladness,
the enemy of mankind.

1272 The poem uses the masculine pronoun *se* instead of the feminine *seo* to refer to Grendel's mother. Some scholars have identified dynamics of gender transgression, perpetuated by the use of the term *aglæcwif*. By referring to Grendel's mother in this way, the original text accentuates her monstrosity by degendering and thus dehumanizing her. For the sake of clarity, our translation uses feminine pronouns.

1280 On the boar-image atop the helmet's crest, see note for line 292.

                              Now his mother,
1270   still ravenous and woeful, would begin
        a sorrowful journey to avenge her son's death.
        She* came to Heorot, where Ring-Danes slept.
        To the men came a change of fortune
        as soon as Grendel's mother broke into the hall.
        Her terror was less, but only by as much
        as the strength of female warriors
        when compared to armed men,
        when a blade, ornamented and hammer-forged,
        the hard, shining sword sweating blood
1280   shears the boar from the helmet's crest.*
        In the hall, sharp-edged swords
        were raised amidst the benches.
        Broad shields were lifted, fixed in hand.
        Both helmets and great coats of mail
        were forgotten when horror overtook the men.
        As soon as Grendel's mother was discovered,
        she was desperate to flee from there
        to preserve her life. Quickly, she seized
        a nobleman and ran toward the fen,
1290   clutching him tight. To Hrothgar, he was
        the best-loved warrior of all the men
        he commanded between the seas,
        a mighty shield-bearer, a glorious man
        whom she slew where he slept.
        Beowulf was not there,
        for other quarters had been provided
        after treasure was given to the renowned Geat.
        Outcry arose in Heorot. She seized
        the famed and gory hand. Grief was renewed
1300   and welled up in that place. It was not
        a good exchange; both parties had paid
        with the lives of friends. Then the old king,
        the aged warrior, was troubled in spirit,

1320 Æschere has been understood to mean "companion," "spear" (as in "one who carries a spear"), or "naval troop." Valentine Anthony Pakis has argued that Æschere, consisting of *æsc* ("ash") and *-here* ("devastation"), is a kenning for "cremation" or "funeral pyre." Frederick Biggs suggests that Hrothgar's naming of Æschere's brother Yrmenlaf ("huge legacy") emphasizes the importance of kin-relationships to the Danes. For Biggs, Hrothgar's emotional response to the death of Æschere stands in stark contrast to the lack of grief that follows Grendel's killing of the Geatish warrior. See Biggs' "Hondscioh and Æschere in *Beowulf*."

for he knew his favorite retainer
was dead, his dearest companion gone.
Beowulf, the victorious one, was quickly fetched
from his private chamber. At the earliest dawn
that noble thane went with his warriors and comrades
to where the wise king waited, wondering
1310   whether the All-Ruling One would ever change
the tidings of woe. The distinguished man
and his troop walked across the floor
– the hall-wood resounded –
until he addressed the wise lord of the Danes.
In light of this urgent summons,
Beowulf asked if his night had been pleasant.

XX.
Hrothgar, protector of the Scyldings, spoke:
"Ask not about happiness. Sorrow
has returned to the men of the Danes.
1320   Æschere is dead, Yrmenlaf's older brother,*
my private counselor and adviser,
shoulder-companion in battle. When warriors
clashed and struck down boar-images,
we protected each other. A warrior ought to be
as Æschere was, foremost in goodness.
This restless, murderous creature became
his hand-slayer in Heorot. I do not know
to where this terrible wretch has fled,
exulting in her kill and gladdened by her feast.
1330   She has revived the feud, for last night
you slew Grendel with the strength
of your hand-grip, since for too long
he diminished and destroyed my men.
He fell in battle, having forfeited his life,
and now comes another scourge of men
wanting to avenge her son, taking retaliation too far,

1339 The word "hand" here could be metonymy for Æschere himself, or, more figuratively, Æschere's service to the king. Leslie Whitbread proposes that Hrothgar is referring to Æschere's actual hand, which has been left by Grendel's mother to avenge the severing of Grendel's hand.

1362 The Old English lines read: *þær mæg nihta gehwæm niðwundor seon, / fyr on flode*. Many scholars have argued that the source of this light is a large fire burning in the center of Grendel's underwater cave (see lines 1522-3). The presence of such a hearth grants hall-like or home-like qualities to Grendel's fen-dwelling. However, others have suggested reading *fyr* as "fiery," which could indicate a supernatural light source other than fire. Or, as *Klaeber 4* notes, "The burning lake or river…is a common feature of European and Asian descriptions of hell."

as it appears to my kinsmen who weep in spirit
for their treasure-giver, terrible heartache.
Now the hand lies dead*
1340   that once fulfilled your every desire.
I have heard said among my people,
land-dwellers and hall-councilors,
that they saw two large creatures such as these
prowling the moors, strange spirits.
One was, from what they could see,
in the likeness of a woman, the other,
a misshapen form traversing the path of exile,
except he was larger than any other man.
In days of yore they called him Grendel;
1350   they knew not of a father, nor whether
any mysterious creatures had been begotten before.
They occupy a wolf-inhabited slope,
secluded in the windy headlands,
which sits at the end of the perilous fen-path,
where the mountain-stream descends
beneath the mist of the cliffs, a flood
under the earth. It is not far from here
that the mere stands. Over it hangs
the frost-covered grove, the fixed roots
1360   of the forest overshadowing the water
where, each night, one may see
a fearful wonder, a fire on the flood.*
No man alive knows its depths.
Even a stag with horns, a heath-rover
chased by dogs, which would prefer
to find refuge in the forest,
having been put to flight from afar,
will first give up its life on the shore of the mere
before daring to seek shelter inside.
1370   That is not a pleasant place.
From there water surges toward the sky,

dark wind stirs up hostile storms
until the air becomes heavy
and the heavens weep.
                           Now, once again
our well-being depends on you alone.
You still do not know the perils
you will encounter in that place.
There you may find a sinful creature;
seek her if you dare. As before,
1380   I will reward you for this fight
with payment of ancient treasures,
coils of gold, if you survive."

XXI.
Beowulf, son of Ecgtheow, spoke:
"Do not grieve, wise man.
For anyone who loses a friend,
it is better to avenge him than mourn too much.
Each of us will experience the end
of this worldly life; may you achieve glory
before death. That is best after the warrior's fall.
1390   Arise, guardian of the kingdom,
let us go now, that we might examine
the track of Grendel's kinswoman.
I promise you she will never find refuge,
neither in the bosom of the earth,
the mountain-wood, nor the ocean's floor,
wherever she decides to go. On this day,
remain patient with each woe,
as I expect you will."
The old king leapt up and thanked
1400   the Mighty Lord for this man's words.
Then Hrothgar's horse, with braided mane,
was bridled. The wise king rode in fine array;
the foot-troop marched, bearing their shields.

1430 We have translated *bewitigað* as "undertake" to convey the sense that the sea-monsters "bring sorrow" to the ships by swimming out and attacking them. Some have understood *bewitigað* to mean "observe," which suggests that the monsters simply watch from the shore as boats shipwreck on the rocks.

Footprints ran along the forest path,
clearly seen, leading directly to the gloomy moor.
Here Grendel's mother had carried
the lifeless form, the best of young retainers who,
with Hrothgar, watched over the homeland.
Now the sons of noblemen walked across
1410   the steep rocky cliffs, narrow ascending paths,
uncharted water-crossings, cragged headlands,
the homes of many water-monsters.
Hrothgar rode in front with a few wise men
to search the ground until he discovered
mountain trees, the joyless wood,
hanging over stones cold and gray.
Water collected beneath, bloody and disturbed.

Grief struck the hearts of the Danes.
The warriors were harrowed when,
1420   on that sea-cliff, they came upon
Æschere's head. The water welled
with blood; the men saw it seething with gore.
A horn sang a desperate war-song.
The foot-troop sank to the ground.
At that moment, they saw a race of serpents
in the water, many strange sea-dragons
exploring the depths, much like the monsters
who lurk on the headland slopes
and undertake sorrow-bringing journeys
1430   on the sail-road at morning-time.*
The creatures fell away, bitter and enraged,
hearing the sharp sound of the singing war-horn.
A man among the Geats used a bow
to deprive a sea-beast of its life;
a stern arrow remained with it, buried
in its innards. It slowed in the water
as death destroyed it. Quickly,

1449 Some Anglo-Saxon helmets, as evinced by the York Helmet (also known as the Coppergate Helmet), included an added layer of protection with a piece of chain-mail hanging from the rear to protect the neck.

1459 Spears and knives were more common weapons than swords in the *Beowulf* poet's era, and a sword such as Unferth's would have been a rare treasure. The sword would have been crafted out of a center iron strip with two steel edges welded to it. The channels left on the faces were filled with layers of twisted and beaten iron and steel, creating an elaborate design.

that strange wave-roamer was pierced
with barbed boar-spears, violently attacked,
1440 and dragged onto the shore.
The men gazed upon this terrible thing.
Unconcerned with the loss of his own life,
Beowulf armed himself with warrior's trappings.
The war-corslet, woven by hand, large
and skillfully decorated, would test the sea.
It knew how to guard his bone-chamber,
so that in battle-grip no malicious grasp
could injure his core. The shining helmet
protected his head. Complete with lordly chains,*
1450 this jewel-studded headgear would stir
the bottom of the mere, diving through
surging waters. As in days past,
the weapon-smith had made the helmet,
furnished it with wondrous things,
adorned it with boar-images, so that no sword
or battle axe could bite through it. Last,
but not least helpful, was the sword lent to the one
in need by Unferth, Hrothgar's court spokesman.
The sword was named Hrunting.*
1460 Preeminent among ancient treasures,
the iron blade, hardened with battle-sweat,
gleamed with intricate designs.
It never failed any man who grasped it
in combat, he who dared to undertake
perilous missions into enemy territory.
It was not the first time this sword was called on
to perform a great work. Surely, mighty Unferth,
son of Ecglaf, did not bear in mind
the wine-drunk words he had spoken before.
1470 Now, he lent his weapon to the better sword-warrior.
Unferth himself did not dare to risk his life
under the wave's turmoil to attempt noble deeds.

Thus he lost glory, his reputation for valor.
The opposite was true for Beowulf
when he armed himself for war.

XXII.
The son of Ecgtheow spoke:
"Hrothgar, renowned son of Healfdane,
wise king and gold-friend of men,
now that I am ready for this undertaking,
1480   remember what we two spoke of before:
if I should lose my life while in your service,
to me, even dead, you will still be as a father.
Be a protector of my young men,
my close comrades, if battle takes me.
Likewise, beloved Hrothgar, send Hygelac
the treasure that you gave me.
When the lord of the Geats, Hrethel's son,
sees this gold, may he gaze upon that precious bounty
and know that I found a good dispenser of rings
1490   and, when I was able, enjoyed his generosity.
And let Unferth have my own hard-edged heirloom,
the splendid wave-patterned sword
widely known to men. With Hrunting
I will achieve fame, or death will carry me off."

After those words, that man of the Weather-Geats
boldly departed; by no means did he wish
to wait for the answer. The surging water
received the warrior. It was the better part of a day
before he could find the bottom.
1500   Before long, she, fiercely ravenous,
the guardian of the sea's expanse
for a hundred half-years, grim and greedy,
perceived a certain foreign creature
exploring the depths of her home.

She reached for the warrior, seized him
in her terrible grip, but she could not
injure his hale body. The armor protected him
from the outside so that she could not
with cunning fingers pierce the war-coat,
1510 the suit of interlinked chains. The she-wolf of the sea
came to the bottom, brought the ring-mailed thane
to her dwelling so he could not,
no matter how courageous, wield his weapons.
Many awful sea-beasts attacked the warrior,
hounded him to such a degree that,
with their battle-tusks, they broke his coat of mail.
Then Beowulf realized that he was
in some kind of cavern, the worst of halls.
No water harmed him in any way
1520 because of the hall's roof;
the sudden rush of the flood could not reach him.
He glimpsed a fiery light, a radiant gleam
brightly shining. The good man saw
the sea-woman, the mighty monster of the deep.
His hand gave a forceful thrust;
it did not withhold the stroke
of the war-sword. His ring-patterned blade
sang a greedy battle-song around her head.
The hall-guest discovered that the iron
1530 could not cut, could not threaten her life.
The swordblade failed the thane in need.
Many before had suffered in hand-to-hand combat
when this weapon would pierce the helmets
and the mail-coats of the doomed.
This was the first time for the noble sword
that its judgment had fallen short.
Still, Hygelac's kinsman was resolute,
intent on his glory and not lacking courage.
The angry warrior tossed the weapon aside.

1551 The Old English reads *Heo him eft hraþe handlean forgeald / grimman grapum ond him togeanes feng*. The word *forgeald* literally means "repaid," making the fight a kind of economic exchange.

1540 The wave-patterned sword, ornamented
   and steel-edged, lay lifeless on the ground.
   Beowulf trusted his strength, the power
   of his hand-grip. In battle, a man should think
   to gain long-lasting fame without care
   for his life. The man of the Geats seized
   Grendel's mother by the shoulder
   – he had no qualms about the feud –
   now enraged, the brave one moved quickly,
   and she, the deadly foe, fell to the floor.
1550 She promptly repaid him with her grim grip
   and seized him.* Tired in spirit,
   the foot-soldier, strongest of warriors,
   stumbled and fell to the ground.
   She charged her hall-visitor again
   and drew her dagger, a broad and shining blade,
   wishing to avenge her offspring, her only son.
   Across Beowulf's shoulder lay
   a woven breast-net; it protected his life
   against sword point and edge, preventing entry.
1560 The Geatish warrior, son of Ecgtheow,
   would have perished under the earth,
   if not for the protection of his armor,
   his coat of mail, and Holy God.
   The wise Lord awarded victory in battle.
   The Ruler of Heaven decided rightly, easily,
   after Beowulf stood up again.

   XXIII.
   He then saw among a collection of weapons
   a victory-blessed sword with strong edges,
   an ancient blade, giant-forged,
1570 glory of warriors. That was the best of weapons
   except it was heavier than any other sword
   that man could carry into battle,

the handiwork of giants, mighty and majestic.
The Scyldings' champion grasped the hilt.
Fierce and sword-grim, he drew
the ring-patterned blade. Despairing,
the brave one viciously struck her,
and the sword slashed through her neck.
Bone-rings broke as the blade sliced through
1580   the doomed body. She fell to the floor.
The sword was covered in blood-sweat;
the man rejoiced in his work. Light shone,
emanating from within, bright as heaven's candle.
Afterwards, he surveyed the cavern, edged
along the wall with his mighty weapon raised.
Hygelac's thane was angry and focused.
This sword would not fail;
the warrior would swiftly repay Grendel
for the many attacks on the Danes,
1590   his numerous raids, and for that time
when he slew Hrothgar's hearth-companions
in their sleep, consumed the slumbering
Danish army, and carried off another
fifteen men, such terrible treasures.
Beowulf, fierce victor, repaid Grendel.
He saw the creature lying drained
in his resting place, lifeless,
for the battle at Heorot had injured him.
The flesh sprang apart when he suffered
1600   a blow after death. With a hard sword stroke,
Beowulf hacked off his head.
The wise men, together with Hrothgar,
gazed at the surging waves, the sea
frothing with shining blood.
The gray-haired ancient ones spoke
of the good thane; they did not expect
his triumphant return to the glorious king.

Many agreed that the she-wolf had torn him apart.
Then came the ninth hour of the day;
1610   the valiant Scyldings left the headlands.
From there the gold-king headed home.
With sad hearts, the Geats sat and gazed at the lake.
They hoped but did not expect to see
their friendly lord again.
                      Then that sword
began to dissolve in battle-sweat,
bloody icicles. That was a strange thing.
The blade waned, melted like ice,
as when the Father releases the fetters of frost,
loosens the frozen waters, He who has power
1620   over season and time. That is the true God.
Though Beowulf saw much there,
he took nothing from that dwelling except
the head and the hilt together, stained treasure.
The sword had melted, the blade
burned up, for the blood was too hot
from the poisonous spirit that died there within.
Soon he was swimming up through the water,
he who survived the fight, the final battle.
A great expanse of surging waves was cleansed
1630   now that the strange spirit had left her life-days
and this temporary world. The protector of seafarers
then came to land, swimming stout-hearted,
exulting in his prize, the mighty load
he carried with him. The valiant troop
rushed toward their leader, thanking God,
rejoicing to see him unharmed. They eagerly
loosened his helmet and mail-coat.
The water subsided, stained with battle-gore
under the skies. From there they went forth,
1640   following footsteps, spirits lifted,
finding the path, the well-known trail.

Two pairs of men, brave as kings,
lugged the head from the sea-cliff
with enormous difficulty. Four were needed
to carry Grendel's head atop the slaughter-pole.
They returned to Heorot, fourteen bold
and valiant Geats marching as a troop
with their courageous leader across the meadow
to the mead-hall. Beowulf came in striding,
1650 the man brave in deeds whose glory brought fame.
The battle-proven thane greeted Hrothgar.
Grendel's head, held by the hair, was dragged
across the floor where men drank, terrible
before the warriors and the queen alike.
All saw a wondrous spectacle.

XXIV.
Beowulf, son of Ecgtheow, spoke:
"*Hwæt*, son of Danes, king of Scyldings,
we gladly bring you this sea-bounty,
this sign of glory that you now behold.
1660 Though I struggled to survive in that fight
under the water, I completed my task.
The battle would have been lost,
had God not protected me.
In the struggle I could not accomplish anything
with Hrunting, though that weapon is mighty.
But the Ruler of Men granted me the sight
of an ancient sword hanging on the wall
– the Mighty One always guides the way
for the friendless – so I drew that blade.
1670 When the opportunity came amidst the fighting,
I slew the guardian of the dwelling.
Then the wave-patterned sword burned up
as the blood spurted forth, hot with battle-sweat.
I claimed the hilt, having avenged

1701 This line in Old English reads *hwam þæt sweord geworht*. Because Old English does not always use prepositions, the word *hwam* could mean either "by whom" or "for whom." Hilda Ellis Davidson has demonstrated that archeological evidence supports both possibilities since researchers have uncovered Anglo-Saxon swords that identify either the maker or the owner. Davidson acknowledges that *hwam* in this line is ambiguous, but she argues that it most likely means "for whom" since *hwam* is not usually used as a dative of agency in Old English.

The construction and decoration of this sword, as described in the poem, have raised some questions. In line 1573 we hear that the sword is "the handiwork of giants" (*giganta geweorc*), but how or why would these giant swordsmiths adorn the hilt with images of their own destruction? Andy Orchard discusses this issue, calling attention to patristic and Irish analogues, in *Pride and Prodigies: Studies in the Monsters of the Beowulf-Manuscript* (pp. 66-85).

violent deeds and Danish deaths,
as was fitting. I promise that now
you will be able to sleep free from care
in Heorot together with your troop of men,
each of your retainers both proven and untried.
1680 Lord of Scyldings, never will you need
to dread the demon-caused death
of your warriors as you did before."
The golden hilt, the ancient work of giants,
was passed to the hand of the old, gray-haired
war-leader. After the fall of the demons,
the work of the wonder-smiths was given
to the Danish king. Once the hostile-hearted
half-man, adversary of God, along with his mother,
departed this world guilty of slaughter,
1690 it came into the power of the worldly king,
the best between the two seas,
he who dispensed silver coins in Scylding lands.
Hrothgar spoke as he examined the sword-hilt,
engraved with the origin of ancient strife
after the rushing flood killed the race of giants
who fared terribly. They were estranged
from the Eternal Lord. He delivered
a flood-surge as final retribution.
Thus, it was rightly engraved in runes
1700 on the hilt's bright golden plates
for whom this weapon was first made.*
It was the best of iron swords, with twisted hilt
and serpentine decoration. Then the wise one,
son of Healfdane, spoke, and all were silent:
"Indeed, an old guardian of the homeland,
one who leads his people with truth
and honor, one who bears the past in mind,
can say that this warrior was born
the greatest of men. Beowulf, my friend,

1718 This is the only mention of someone named Ecgwela as one of the founders of the Danish nation. Kemp Malone proposes that because *ecg-wela* ("sword-vexer") could be a kenning for "shield," this may be another way of referring to Scyld Scefing. For Heremod, see note for line 864.

1722 The poet says that Heremod was sent away from *mon-dreamum*. This compound noun is literally translated as "man-joys," which could refer both to the happiness afforded to members of the human race and, more significantly, to the fact that such happiness requires social interaction.

1710   your fame has been established
       throughout distant regions, across every nation.
       You carry yourself with composure,
       tempering your strength with skill of mind.
       As I had pledged, I will stand by my friendship.
       You must become a long-lasting comfort
       to your people, a help to mankind,
       unlike Heremod to the Honor-Scyldings,
       the sons of Ecgwela.* He did not flourish into favor
       but brought violent death to Danish men.
1720   Inflamed with rage, he killed his table-mates
       until the infamous lord had to turn alone
       from the joys of life among men,*
       though the mighty God had granted him strength,
       blessed him with power, and promoted him
       above all others. However, the bloodthirst
       in his spirit grew; he gave rings to no one
       in spite of Danish custom. He remained joyless.
       For his crimes he suffered the long-lasting
       punishment demanded by his people.
1730   From this story, learn the virtue of generosity.
       With the wisdom of many winters,
       I tell you this tale. It is incredible
       how the glorious God gives prudence,
       land, and rank to the race of men
       with benevolent spirit. He possesses
       power over all. At times He allows
       the mind of an illustrious man to be moved
       by his desires. He gives him the joys of the earth
       in his native land, governance over his community.
1740   He makes broad portions of the world
       subject to this man, who, for his lack of wisdom,
       cannot conceive of his end. This man lives
       only to feast. Illness by no means impairs him,
       neither old age nor dire sorrow darken his mind,

XXV There is enjambment between fitts as Fitt XXV begins with the subordinating conjunction *oð þæt* ("until"), which connects its opening line to the final line of Fitt XXIV.

1753 "The slayer" is the devil. As Mark Atherton has demonstrated, the image of the devil shooting arrows was used to represent temptation in the patristic tradition and in Anglo-Saxon religious texts. The metaphor derives from St. Paul's letter to the Ephesians 6.

1778 This litany of the ways in which a man could die uses a grammatical construction that does not appear elsewhere in the poem, but *Klaeber 4* points out that the repetition of *oððe* (equivalent to Modern English "or") in similar types of lists is common in Old English homilies. The Old English reads:

> *eft sona bið*
> *þæt þec adl oððe ecg   eafoþes getwæfeð,*
> *oððe fyres feng,   oððe flodes wylm,*
> *oððe atol yldo;   oððe eagena bearhtm*
> *forsiteð ond forsworceð;   semninga bið*
> *þæt ðec, dryhtguma,   deað oferswyðeð.*

nor do strife or sword-hate occur,
but the whole world goes according to his will.
He does not know worse

XXV.*
until a large measure of arrogance
waxes and flourishes within him,
1750 when his conscience, the keeper of souls,
sleeps. Its rest is too deep, bound in distress,
and the slayer is very near,
he who shoots from a bow with evil intent.*
Then the man is hit in his breast, wounded
below his helmet with a sharp arrow.
He does not know how to protect himself
from the perverse temptations
of the accursed demon. It appears to him
that all the things he long guarded
1760 are not enough; the hostile-minded man
becomes greedy. To his shame,
he never gives gold-plated rings. He forgets
and disregards both his future destiny
and what God, Lord of Glory, had given him,
his portion of worldly honor. In the end
the fleeting body withers, fated to die,
and he falls. A new ruler takes the treasures
and liberally shares the spoils of the late king
without fear or hesitation. Protect against
1770 mortal affliction, beloved Beowulf, greatest of men,
and seek the good, choose eternal benefits.
Do not give in to prideful thoughts, renowned warrior.
Now, in this moment, you are in your prime.
But soon you will be deprived of your strength,
whether in the grip of fire, or the surge of a flood,
the attack of the sword, or the flight of a spear,
or even in the terror of old age, the brightness
of your eyes will fail and grow dim.*

1802 The word in Old English here is *nihthelm* ("night-helmet"). It appears elsewhere in Old English texts to figuratively refer to night. The use of "helmet" invokes the notion of the sky as a dome and also implies a sense of protection in darkness. As Chickering notes, the appearance of *nihthelm* at this point in the poem is significant because, following Beowulf's defeat of Grendel and Grendel's mother, night is once again a time of safety for the Danes (p. 345).

Soon, warrior, death will overpower you.
1780 I have ruled the Ring-Danes under the skies
for a hundred half-years. With ash-wood spears
and swordblades I have protected them in wars
against many nations throughout the world.
I did not consider any challenger under the heavens
to be a threat. What a change of fortune
came into my native land! Sorrow replaced joy
when Grendel, the ancient adversary,
became my enemy. I long bore the grief
of endless persecution. Therefore, thanks be to God,
1790 the Eternal Lord, that I lived to see this,
that I can, after the old turmoil,
gaze upon that gore-drenched head.
Go now to your seat, take joy in feasting,
for you have distinguished yourself in battle.
In the morning a great many treasures
will be shared among us." The Geatish man
was glad in mind, and turned at once
to seek his seat, as the wise king had commanded.

Now it was again as it was before.
1800 A new feast was prepared
for the brave men sitting in the hall.
The dark helmet of night* descended
upon the warriors. The men all stood;
the gray-haired king, ancient Scylding,
wished to sleep. The shield-warrior,
brave Geat, sorely wanted rest.
A hall-retainer led the way for him.
Beowulf was exhausted, having come from afar.
Out of courtesy, the retainer attended
1810 to all of his needs, just as sea-warriors
were expected to do in those days.
The great-hearted one rested.

[1768-1799]   109

1815 The raven is usually associated with death, but some folk traditions celebrated the raven as a morning bird and a good omen. The poet describes the bird as a *hrefn blaca*, which may be a form of the Old English word for "black" (*blæc*) or for "bright" (*blac*). For discussion of this morning scene, see Kathryn Hume's "The Function of the *Hrefn Blaca*: *Beowulf* 1801" and Chickering, pp. 344-7.

The gabled and gold-adorned hall towered.
The guest slept until the black raven,
merry at heart, proclaimed heaven's joy.*
When light advanced over the shadows,
the warriors hastened; the noblemen
were eager to return to their people
once more. The bold-hearted thane wished
1820   to seek out his ship, to sail to his faraway home.
Beowulf, the brave one, then commanded
that Hrunting be brought to the son of Ecglaf.
He bade him take back his precious iron-sword.
Beowulf thanked Unferth for this loan
and told him he considered the sword
a good war-friend, strong in battle.
He made no mention of the sword's failure.
That was a gracious man.
The warriors in their armor were eager to depart.
1830   The nobleman honored by the Danes walked
to the throne where the other leader sat.
The proven hero addressed Hrothgar.

XXVI.
Beowulf, son of Ecgtheow spoke:
"Now we seafarers, having come from afar,
wish to say that we are eager to return
to Hygelac. Here we were properly entertained
according to our wishes; you have treated us well.
Lord of men, if there is anything on earth
I can do beyond my recent war-deeds
1840   to earn your love, I will be ready immediately.
If I ever hear from across the sea
that neighboring peoples threaten you with war,
as hostile nations have sometimes done,
I will bring one thousand warriors to help.
I know that Hygelac, lord of the Geats,

1853 The Old English reads *Feorcyþðe beoð / selran gesohte þæm þe him selfa deah.* This appears to be an idiomatic expression that offers a few possibilities for translation. According to *Klaeber 4*, the sentence might literally mean "far countries when visited (i.e., travels to far countries) are good for him who will do right for himself," and scholars have noted similar maxims that appear in Old Norse texts. Rather than simply extolling the virtues of travel, however, Beowulf may be advising Hrethric to behave morally because a righteous man will have an easier time getting along in a foreign country. In "Reading *Beowulf* with Original Eyes" James Earl suggests that Beowulf is predicting Hrethric's treachery and here is saying that "a man who would save himself had best seek distant friends."

guardian of our people, young though he may be,
wishes to support me with words and work,
so I can rightly honor you and bring to you
a forest of spears when you are in need of men.
1850 If your son Hrethric decides to come
to the court of the Geats, there your kinsman
will find many friends. Distant friends
are better sought by he who acts with honor."*
Hrothgar replied: "The wise Lord sent
those words into your heart. Never in my life
have I heard such a young man speak so well.
Not only do you have great strength,
but you are also wise in spirit, wise in words.
If it comes to pass that Hygelac, son of Hrethel,
1860 the leader and guardian of your people,
is taken by grim war, spear, illness, or iron-sword,
and you keep your life, I am convinced
that the Geats could not choose a better king,
a better guardian of the treasure-hoard, than you,
should you wish to rule the realm of your kinsmen.
Beloved Beowulf, the longer I know you,
the more your character pleases me.
You have made it so that Geats and Danes
will nurture mutual peace and lay to rest
1870 conflict, the enmity previously harbored.
As long as I rule the broad kingdom,
there will be shared treasure, and many will greet
one another with goods across the sea-bird's bath.
The curved-prow ship shall bring gifts
and tokens of affection over the water.
I know our nations will stand together,
both with friends and against enemies,
in every way blameless as it used to be."

Then, inside the hall, the warrior's protector,

1880   Hrothgar, gave twelve treasures to Beowulf.
      He commanded him to go safely with his gifts
      to his own people and to return soon.
      The noble king of the Scyldings kissed
      the greatest of thanes and embraced him.
      Tears fell from the gray-haired man.
      Ancient and wise, he envisioned
      two possibilities, the more likely being
      that they would never see each other again,
      as they were then, brave men in discourse.
1890   Beowulf was so dear to him that he could not
      hold back the tears welling in his breast;
      his deep attachment to that noble man,
      fixed in his heart's bond, burned in his blood.
      Beowulf, the gold-proud warrior,
      walked away from him on the grassy land,
      exulting in his treasures. The ship awaited
      its master, swaying on its anchor.
      On their way to the water, the gifts of Hrothgar
      were frequently praised. That was one king
1900   who was altogether blameless until old age
      drained his strength, as it always does.

      XXVII.
      Then the troop of spirited young men
      came to the shore in their coats of woven ring-mail.
      Hrothgar's shore-guardian watched the arrival
      of the warriors as he had done before.
      He did not greet them from the cliff
      with insults but instead rode toward them
      and said that they would be welcomed home
      in Geatland, these bright-mailed warriors
1910   who were marching to their vessel.
      The lofty, curved-prow ship on the shore
      was laden with armor, horses, and treasures;

1941 It is not uncommon for characters in *Beowulf* to have compounded names (Ecg-theow, Wulf-gar, Hyge-lac) that function like kennings, which may provide the audience with insight into the character. The name of Hygd is less telling than others. Alone, her name means "mind," and as a counterpart to her husband, Hygelac (see note for line 193), we might read her name as "mind without strife."

the high mast towered above the gifts
from Hrothgar's hoard. Beowulf gave
a sword bound in gold to the ship-guard,
who afterwards became a more honored man
on the mead-bench with this heirloom treasure.
The ship began to stir up the deep water
and left the land of the Danes. The sail,
1920   the ship's sea-garment, was fixed
to the mast with rope; the planks creaked.
By no means did the wind over the water
hinder the voyage of the wave-floater.
The sea-walker set out, the foamy-necked ship
sailed across sea currents, until the men
could see the Geatish cliffs, familiar headlands.
The ship surged onward, driven ashore by the wind.
The harbor-guard was ready at the water's edge,
he who had long watched the tide
1930   for his dear companions. He secured
the broad-beamed ship on the shore,
fixed with anchor ropes, lest the force
of the waves dash the splendid vessel to pieces.
He then commanded that the noblemen's
treasure, garments, and plated gold
be brought ashore. It was not far from there
that the giver of treasure, Hygelac,
son of Hrethel, lived with his retainers
near the shore. The building was stately;
1940   the powerful king was in the high hall.
His young wife Hygd* was wise and virtuous,
though she had lived but a few years
in the royal stronghold. That queen,
daughter of Hæreth, was not meager,
nor too frugal with gifts of treasure
to the men of the Geats. Another queen,
Fremu, acted with arrogance, committed

1948 Where many previous translations of *Beowulf* use the name Modthryth or Thrytho for the bad queen, we agree with Robert Fulk's argument that the name of this queen is Fremu. For discussion of this famous textual crux, see the note for line 1931b in *Klaeber 4* and Fulk's "The Name of Offa's Queen: *Beowulf* 1931-2."

1957 The Old English word *freoðuwebbe* means "peace-weaver" and is indicative of the expected role of an Anglo-Saxon queen. A royal woman would be given in marriage to the leader of another tribe or nation in order to secure a political alliance. As a member of her new community, the queen would signify the friendly bond between tribes and would serve as a pacifying presence among the warriors in the hall.

1960 The story of Offa and Fremu has been seen as an example of the Taming of the Shrew motif, which was rehearsed in a variety of legends and most famously staged by Shakespeare in the sixteenth century.

For the initial audience of *Beowulf*, the name Offa may have invoked two historical counterparts, accounts of whom are presented in a variety of sources. In the early thirteenth century, these accounts were compiled into a Latin text, the *Vitae duorum Offarum* (*Lives of the Two Offas*). Offa I was a legendary king of the Angles who may have ruled in North Frisia in the fourth century; he is celebrated as a great warrior-king in the Old English poem *Widsith*. Offa II ruled the kingdom of Mercia in England from 757 to 796. Until the ninth-century reign of Alfred the Great, he was the most powerful of the Anglo-Saxon kings.

1976 Eomer, Hemming, and Garmund are mentioned in genealogies as members of the royal family of Mercia, an English kingdom established by the Angles.

terrible crimes.* None of the court-retainers,
dear as they were, dared to gaze upon her
1950 in daylight, unless he was a great lord,
for if he did, he could count on deadly bonds
ordered for him, twisted by hand;
he would be arrested immediately.
A patterned sword would be chosen
to settle the matter and deliver the death-blow.
This is not a queenlike custom for a woman,
beautiful as she may be, for a peace-weaver*
to deprive a dear man of life on account of
her own pretended injury. King Offa
1960 stopped her.* Indeed, other ale-drinkers said
that she inflicted less harm upon people,
fewer hostile acts, when, adorned in gold,
she was given to the young champion.
She became dear to the nobility
after making the journey to the hall of Offa
across the glinting sea, according to her father's wishes.
There, she fared well on the throne,
glorious in her grace, making good use of her life.
She honored Offa, this chief of warriors,
1970 with great esteem. I have heard that he
was the best king between the two seas.
This spear-bold man was honored far and wide
for his gift-giving and battle-prowess.
With wisdom he guarded his native land.
From him sprung Eomer, kinsman of Hemming,
nephew of Garmund, help to heroes, powerful in battle.*

XXVIII.
Beowulf walked with his troop of retainers
along the sandy shore, traversing the wide coast.
The world-candle shone, the eager southern sun.
1980 They had completed their journey.

[1933-1966]

1983 Ongentheow was the king of the Swedes who was defeated in battle with the Geats. After his brother Hæthcyn fell, Hygelac led the Geatish troops, but he did not kill Ongentheow himself. Beowulf will recall this battle in lines 2468-2500.

They boldly went to where they had heard
that the young war-king Hygelac,
their protector, the slayer of Ongentheow,*
was sitting inside the stronghold distributing rings.
Hygelac was soon informed of Beowulf's return:
the protector of warriors had returned from battle,
alive and unharmed, and he was heading
toward the court with his comrades.
Quickly the hall was cleared for the soldiers,
1990　as the mighty one had commanded.
Beowulf, having survived the fight,
sat opposite the king, kinsman with kinsman,
after the lord of men addressed the loyal one
with proper and earnest words.
Hygd, daughter of Hæreth, glided
through the great hall with cups of mead.
She cared for the people, bearing strong drink
to the hands of the troops. Hygelac began
to question his thane inside the high hall,
2000　courteous yet eager to know how
the Sea-Geats had fared on their journey:
"What happened to you on that venture,
dear Beowulf, after you abruptly decided
to seek a fight at Heorot across the salty sea?
Did you in any way remedy the widely known
troubles of Hrothgar, the renowned king?
I have brooded over your expedition
with surging sorrow and heavy grief,
for I did not have great confidence in you,
2010　my dear thane. I long urged you
not to challenge that murderous creature
and, instead, to allow the Danes
to settle the feud with Grendel themselves.
I give thanks to God for allowing your safe return."
Beowulf, son of Ecgtheow, spoke:

2038 The poem does not previously mention Freawaru. The meaning of her name is unclear.

2041 Beowulf begins to foreshadow Ingeld's eventual betrayal of the truce between the Danes and the Heathobards, a truce bound by the peace-pledge of Freawaru, Hrothgar's daughter. After the breaking of this truce, Ingeld and the Heathobards will attack Hrothgar and Hrothulf on Danish land. Although the Danes will defeat the Heathobards, the battle will result in the destruction of Heorot, as mentioned in lines 84-7. This feud is narrated in the Anglo-Saxon poem *Widsith*, as well as by Saxo Grammaticus in his twelfth-century *Gesta Danorum*.

2048 Heathobards means "war-beards."

"That famous encounter is no secret among men,
Lord Hygelac, the battle that occurred
between me and Grendel in the hall
where he had inflicted a great many sorrows,
2020 ceaseless miseries, on the Victory-Scyldings.
These I avenged so none of Grendel's kinsmen,
not one on earth, even the longest-living
of that hateful race enveloped in sin,
would ever boast of that night's struggle.
I first went into the ring-hall to greet Hrothgar.
After learning of my intentions,
the famed son of Healfdane offered me a seat
next to his own sons. The company was joyful;
never have I seen under heaven's vault
2030 a greater troop sitting in a hall rejoicing
with mead. The renowned queen,
peace-pledge between nations,
would walk throughout the hall,
encouraging the young men, giving
them rings before returning to her seat.
At times, Hrothgar's daughter also
bore the ale-cup to the gathered warriors.
I heard the men call her Freawaru*
when she offered them the jeweled goblet.
2040 She, young and adorned in gold, has been
promised to Ingeld, the gracious son of Froda.*
The lord of the Scyldings, keeper of the kingdom,
accepts wise advice, and so he will settle his part
of the deadly feud by offering this woman.
It rarely happens after a nation's defeat
that the spear remains idle for long,
no matter how well the bride performs.
It may offend the lord of the Heathobards*
and each of his men, his retainers,
2050 when the well-born son of the Danes

XXIX The manuscript indicates the start of a new fitt with a capital "O" in *oððæt*, but there is no corresponding Roman numeral. The manuscript also does not include a marker for the start of Fitt XXX and so the numbering skips to XXXI.

2071 Withergyld was presumably one of the Heathobard leaders. His name has a sense of requital or recompense; it literally means "hostile-gold," or gold paid to one's enemy.

walks into their hall to formally present the bride.
The heirlooms of ancestors gleam on him,
brave and ring-adorned; these had been
the treasures of the Heathobards
while they were yet able to wield weapons

[XXIX.]*

until they led themselves and their comrades
to destruction in shield-play. Then,
at the banquet, an old warrior speaks,
he who sees the shining weapons
2060   and remembers all too well
how his comrades died by the spear;
his is a grim spirit. Sad at heart,
he begins to test a young warrior's character,
to examine his heart-thoughts, to awaken
the evil of war, and he makes this speech:
'Can you, my friend, recognize the blade
that your father carried into battle
under his war-mask for the last time,
his beloved iron-sword? There,
2070   the Danes slew him, the Scylding heroes
controlled the battlefield when Withergyld*
lay dead after our valiant soldiers had fallen.
Now, here, one of those killers' sons
strides into the hall exulting in treasure,
boasting of murder and wearing the jewels
that are rightly yours.' The old man presses so
and reminds the young man of these things
with bitter words, until the time comes
that one of the bride's retainers,
2080   because of his father's violent deeds,
is bloodstained and asleep in death,
cut by the sword, having forfeited his life.
The avenger escapes from there, alive;
he knows the land well. On both sides

2091 Beowulf's speech reflects the oral tradition of the time in its flattery and measured boasts, but note the discrepancies between Beowulf's narration of his battles and what was earlier described in the poem.

2098 Beowulf here names for the first time the Geat warrior who was killed in line 706. Hondscio means "hand-shoe," or "glove."

2108 The word in Old English is *glof*, which becomes the modern "glove," and can refer to a bag or pouch. There is a clear linguistic connection between *handscio* and Grendel's *glof*. For one consideration of the significance of this, see Seth Lerer's article "Grendel's Glove."

the oaths of the warriors are broken
after the deadly rage swells in Ingeld.
Because of grief, his affection for his wife
grows cold. I do not consider the loyalty
of the Heathobards, their part in the alliance
2090 with the Danes, to be sincere, nor their friendship firm.

Now I will speak further about Grendel,*
so that you will know well, ring-giver,
what resulted from the heroes' hand-combat.
After the jewel of heaven had moved
across the earth, the angry creature came,
hideous night-demon, to seek us where we,
still unharmed, occupied the hall.
There was a fatal attack on Hondscio,*
our fellow warrior. Deadly evil doomed him.
2100 He was the first to die. Grendel became
the mouth-slayer of that dear young man
and devoured his entire body.
Moments later, empty-handed,
the bloody-toothed murderer, intent
on evil, wished to leave that gold-hall
but he, in his boldness, tested the limits
of my strength. Primed, he struck.
The corpse-bag* hung, large and strange,
skillfully sewn, and masterfully assembled
2110 with demons' craft and dragon's hide.
He, the ferocious doer of evil deeds,
wished to place me, guiltless, there
inside the sack, one of many victims.
It could not be so, for I leapt up in fury.
It would take too long to recount
how I repaid that scourge of men
with a hand-blow for each evil,
and how, my king, I honored your people

with my deeds. He escaped down a path
2120 and clung to life for a short while. Yet,
his right hand remained behind in Heorot
to mark his track, while he, humiliated
and sad in spirit, died at the bottom of the mere.
The lord of the Scyldings rewarded me
with much gold and many treasures
when morning came and we sat down
to the feast. There was story and song:
Hrothgar, the ancient Scylding,
with his store of great knowledge
2130 recounted tales from long ago.
At times, the warrior-king played the harp,
the joyful strings. He recited a true and tragic song.
Later, the great-hearted king skillfully narrated
a strange and wondrous tale. After a while,
the ancient Hrothgar, bound by his old age,
began to lament his battle-strong youth.
He soon welled up inside when he,
wise in winters, remembered all that he had known.
We celebrated the entire day until another night fell.
2140 The mother of Grendel was ready for vengeance,
so she made a sorrow-bringing journey; death
had destroyed her son in battle with the Geats.
The monstrous mother avenged her son
and brazenly killed a warrior. Life departed
from Æschere, that counselor of old.
After morning came, the men of the Danes
were not able to burn the death-weary body,
nor lay their beloved man on a funeral pyre.
She ran off below the mountain stream,
2150 his body clutched in the enemy's embrace.
For Hrothgar, that was the most crushing of sorrows
that had befallen him for a long time.
In your name, the anguished king asked that

2183 Heorogar was Hrothgar's older brother who preceded Hrothgar as king of the Scyldings. It appears that Heorogar gave this breastplate to Hrothgar, and this may have coincided with Heorogar likewise passing the throne to Hrothgar instead of to his eldest son, Heoroweard. Hrothgar giving the breastplate to Hygelac through Beowulf signals the importance of the relationship between the Scyldings and the Geats.

I perform this heroic deed in the tossing waves,
risking my life and affirming my glory.
He promised to reward me.
It is widely known that I, in the churning water,
found the grim, terrible, guardian of the deep.
For a while we were hand-to-hand
2160 and the water frothed with gore.
In that fen-hall, using a mighty sword,
I chopped off the head of Grendel's mother.
Against great odds, I escaped from that place
with my life; I was not yet fated to die.
Hrothgar, the protector of warriors and son of Healfdane,
afterwards presented me with many treasures.

XXXI.
Thus the king of the Scyldings abided by tradition.
I have not lost those gifts, rewards for my strength.
Hrothgar also gave me treasures of my own choosing
2170 that I now wish to bring and bestow upon you,
with good will, king of warriors. Still,
all of my happiness is dependent on you;
I have few close kinsmen except for you, Hygelac."

Beowulf ordered that a banner with a boar-image,
a tall helmet, a silver mail-coat, and a splendid
war-sword be brought inside. He gave a speech:
"The wise lord Hrothgar gave me this armor.
He commanded that I first explain
the history of these gifts. He said that
2180 King Heorogar of the Scyldings had owned
the breast-plate for a long while, yet
he never wished to give it to Heoroweard,
his valiant son, though he was loyal.*
Take joy in these gifts."
I heard that four horses, all alike,

2195 This is the neck-ring discussed in lines 1183-1202.

2215 Hrethel was the father of Hygelac and the previous king of the Geats. Like Heorogar's gift of his breastplate to Hrothgar, Hygelac's gifting of this sword symbolizes a bestowal of political power upon Beowulf, a power he will be allowed to exercise on his own lands. For discussion of the ritualized exchange of gifts between Beowulf and Hygelac, see Frederick Biggs, "The Politics of Succession in *Beowulf* and Anglo-Saxon England" and Erin Mullally, "Hrethel's Heirloom: Kinship, Succession, and Weaponry in *Beowulf*."

2219 In Anglo-Saxon England, a *hid* was an area of land believed to be large enough to support a household, but it did not have a fixed measurement. According to *Klaeber 4*, Beowulf receives a territory of approximately 890 square miles (2300 sq. km.).

tawny and swift, came along with the treasure.
With good will, he offered both steeds and war-gear.
This is how a kinsman should act: he must never
weave a net of malice with secret cunning
2190 to plot the death of a comrade. To the battle-hard
Hygelac, Beowulf was a loyal nephew;
each was mindful of the other's well-being.
I heard that he gave Hygd the neck-ring,
the beautiful ornament that Wealhtheow,
daughter of a king, had given to him,*
and three graceful horses with bright saddles.
Since then, Hygd's breast was adorned with that ring.
Thus Beowulf, a man famous for battle,
proved himself with good deeds.
2200 He pursued honor and never struck
his hearth-companions after drinking.
He did not have a wicked temper,
and the battle-brave man controlled
the extraordinary gift God had given him:
the greatest strength of all mankind.
For a long time he had been mistreated,
as the Geats did not deem him worthy,
nor did their lord wish to give him
many gifts among the mead-benches.
2210 They truly thought him to be inept,
a feeble nobleman. For each indignity
a reversal of fortune came to that glorious man.
Then Hygelac, the lord of warriors,
the battle-brave king, bade them bring in
Hrethel's gold-adorned heirloom.*
At that time, a better sword could not be found
among the treasure of the Geats.
This he laid on Beowulf's lap and gave him
seven thousand hides of land,* a hall,
2220 and a throne. Together they owned

2232 The poet here fast-forwards through the events that lead to Beowulf eventually ascending to the Geatish throne. Details about these battles will be provided in a series of flashbacks throughout the rest of the poem. According to Gregory of Tours' sixth-century *Historia Francorum* (*History of the Franks*), a Danish king named Hygelac led a disastrous raid into Gaul around 520.

2237 The dragon's barrow is positioned close to the sea on the edge of a cliff. The mound resembles actual burial mounds found in Britain and Scandinavia. A stream flows from the entrance, which is marked by two stone slabs. The entrance leads to a passageway that opens into a central chamber containing the dragon's hoard, an assortment of jewels, goblets, and weapons.

2239 The manuscript is badly damaged here, so editors have had to accept that much of this narrative has been lost and conjecture what the poem probably said. Many words cannot be clearly discerned on the manuscript or are missing altogether. Words inside brackets reflect scholars' best efforts to reconstruct the poem. The ellipses indicate places where the manuscript is so damaged that scholars cannot even guess what the poem said.

2249 There is some contention about who this man is. The letter *thorn* (þ) is visible here, but none of the letters afterwards, allowing for *þeow* "slave," *þegn* "thane, retainer," or *þeof* "thief." Some have argued that the thief was a nobleman who offended his lord and had to flee, so he stole from the dragon's treasure in order to pay off his offense. Alternately, the thief could have been a common man who was simply stealing to pay off debt or the price owed for a previous crime.

inherited land in that nation, ancestral property,
but the larger kingdom remained in the hands
of Hygelac, the man of higher rank.
In later days, it came to pass that,
after the battle-clash in which Hygelac was killed,
and swords became the slayers of Heardred
even under the protection of shields,
when strong Swedish warriors pursued him
among his proud people and struck down
2230 the nephew of Hereric, the broad kingdom
was passed to the hand of Beowulf.
He ruled it well for fifty winters*
– he was a wise king,
old guardian of the homeland –
until another began to reign in the dark of nights,
a dragon who guarded its hoard in a great
but distant place, a steep stone barrow.*
The ascending path lay hidden to men.
One man ventured inside and seized [...]*
2240 from the heathen hoard, his hand
[took a cup] shining with gems.
[It] afterwards [avenged] – or, [did not hide]
[though] sleeping [it was tricked]
with thief's cunning. [The people discovered],
the nation of warriors, that the dragon was enraged.

XXXII.
Not at all by choice, not of his own will
did the man [break into] the dragon's hoard
with his craft, he who injured the dragon.
The [servant of a certain nobleman]*
2250 fled the hostile blows of the sons of men
and, [in need of refuge], entered therein,
that man burdened by sin. Soon it happened
that [...] horror rose in the intruder.

2255 The manuscript is almost completely obscured here. The word *sceapen* ("created") is visible twice, but scholars have been unsuccessful at discerning any other words. While inconvenient, the loss of the text is fittingly located during a theft, the loss of the treasure.

2274 This brief elegy (lines 2274-96) is commonly referred to as The Lay of the Last Survivor.

However [........] created [........]
[...................] created [...........]*
[....................] fear grew in him,
he who had sought the precious cup.
There were many such ancient relics
inside that earth-hall, since in days of yore
2260   some unknown man, after careful consideration,
had hidden there the vast wealth
of his noble nation, their precious treasures.
Death had already carried off his people,
and the one of that nation who still lived,
the guardian in mourning, expected
the same for himself, knowing he would
only be able to enjoy those ancient treasures,
long-accumulated, for a short time.
The barrow stood ready on a plateau
2270   near the waves of the sea, newly-prepared
on the headland, craftily secured.
This guardian of rings placed inside there
a portion of the golden treasure worthy
of being hoarded. He spoke a few words:*
"Hold you now, Earth, since men may not,
this treasure of past nobles, what was
once claimed by brave ones. Battle-death
destroyed them, this fearful and deadly attack
on each of my people who left this life,
2280   those who had seen the joys of the hall.
I have no one to bear the gold-plated sword,
or [carry] my gold cup, my precious drinking-vessel.
My companions have gone.
The hard helmet, decorated with gold,
will lose its brilliance; the polisher
who would shine the helmet sleeps in death.
Likewise, the coat of armor that had, in battle,
endured the crashing cut of swords across shields

2307 While the *Beowulf* poet uses the masculine pronoun "he" to refer to the drag-on, we use the gender-neutral "it" because, unlike Grendel and Grendel's mother, who possess a certain degree of humanity, the dragon is clearly a beast. We use "it" to distinguish the dragon from its human adversaries.

will decay after the warrior. The chain-mail
2290   will no longer travel with the war-chief,
who once had journeyed with a troop by his side.
Nowhere does the sweet harp sound,
no strings dance. No high hawk soars
through the hall, no swift steed stamps
the grounds. Cruel death has stolen
many men from this world." So,
with a mournful mind, he spoke of sorrow.
Joyless and alone, one man after all had gone,
he wandered day and night,
2300   until death's flood engulfed his heart.

The ravager who comes before dawn,
the burning one who seeks barrows,
found the hoard standing open.
The malicious dragon, unadorned,
flies by night, dressed only in flame;
earth-dwellers [were terrified of it].
It* will claim a hoard in the earth, where,
old in winters, it guards its heathen gold,
but is in no way better for it.
2310   For three hundred years that dreaded one,
terrible in its power, held a hoard in the ground
until one man angered its spirit. The thief
carried the gold-plated cup to his lord
and pled for peace. The treasure had been
ransacked, the hoard of rings plundered,
and mercy was granted to the wretched man.
The king examined the artifact for the first time.

Then the dragon awoke and the feud
was rekindled. Sniffing along the stones,
2320   the hard-hearted one discovered the track
of its enemy. With cunning, the thief

2338 The Old English verb *forgyldan*, which we have rendered "avenge," typically refers to monetary compensation rather than violent retribution (see note to line 1551). The dragon wants to be paid for the cup, but the price it wishes to exact is that it will set fire to the thief or his property.

had stealthily crept near the dragon's head.
An undoomed man can easily survive misery
and exile, he who holds the favor of the Lord.
The guardian of the hoard scoured the ground,
determined to find the man who had wronged it
while it slept. Full of heat and rage,
it circled the outside of the barrow over
and over. There was no man to be found
2330   in that wasteland, yet it thirsted for battle,
the work of war. At times it returned to the barrow
in search of the precious cup. It soon found
that some man had disturbed its gold,
its beloved treasure. Anxious, the guardian
of the hoard waited until the evening came.
The enraged keeper of the barrow, the hated foe,
wished to avenge the dear drinking cup
with flame.* The day finally passed.
The dragon could remain within the wall no longer,
2340   so it burst forth in flame, impelled by fire.
This was a terrible beginning for the men on land,
and for Beowulf, the treasure-giver,
it would soon lead to a grievous end.

XXXIII.

The unwelcome guest began to spew flame,
burning the splendid court; fire-light erupted
as a terror to men. The hostile night-glider
wished to leave nothing alive.
The dragon's attack was seen throughout the land,
the fury of the enemy from near and far,
2350   how that scourge of Geatish men
assailed and injured them. It hastened
back to the hoard, to its fine hidden hall
before daybreak. It held the people
in the grip of fire, flame and blaze.

2360 The word we have rendered as "throne" is *gifstol*. Literally translated as "gift-seat," this would be the place from which a king would distribute treasure to his subjects.

2376 Although Anglo-Saxon shields were made of a variety of materials, they were most commonly made of linden wood, also called lime wood. It was likely favored for its versatility, as it is soft and easily worked.

2388 The word *forgrap*, rendered here as "crushed," recalls the battle with Grendel in which Beowulf used his powerful grip.

The dragon trusted in the barrow, in its own
fighting prowess, and the cave's stone walls.
Its expectation would prove false.
The terror was soon made known to Beowulf
that his own home, his finest hall,
2360   the throne of the Geats,* was consumed
by surges of fire. That good man felt grief
in his heart, the deepest of sorrows.
Beowulf, in his wisdom, thought that
he had broken the ancient law of the Ruler,
that he had sorely offended the Eternal Lord.
Dark thoughts welled from within his breast,
which he was not accustomed to.
The fire-dragon had burned to ash
the stronghold of the people, which had stood
2370   in the place where the earth meets the sea.
The war-king, protector of the Geats,
plotted revenge. The lord commanded
his warriors to make a shield entirely of iron,
a wondrous battle-guard; he knew well
his wooden shield could not protect him,
linden against flame.* This prince and seafarer,
great for so long, must face the end of his days,
this worldly life, together with the dragon,
the one who had long held the hoard.
2380   The king scorned the aid of a company,
a great army, in seeking the far-flier.
Beowulf himself did not dread battle,
nor did he think much of the dragon's power,
its strength and courage, because he had survived
many conflicts, triumphed in storms of war,
since the time that he, the man of many victories,
had cleansed Hrothgar's hall, and, in combat,
crushed Grendel and his kin,* that hated race.
Not the least of his feats took place

2390 Hygelac pays the ultimate price for his aggression and overconfidence as he dies while attacking Frisia. During the battle, Beowulf again performs extraordinary feats, but his individual success is somewhat tempered by the Geats' loss of their king and the problem of royal succession.

2398 The Old English proper noun *Hetwaras* could refer to the Chattuarii, a Frankish tribe that occupied land in what is now northwestern Germany, or it might be another term for the Frisians.

2416 After Heardred takes the throne, he takes in the brothers Eanmund and Eadgils (sons of the late Swedish king Ohthere), who were exiled from Sweden after attempting to overthrow their uncle, Onela (who is married to Hrothgar's daughter, as mentioned in line 65). Onela leads an army to Geatland, where he kills Heardred. Beowulf is then made ruler of the Geats. More details of this battle, including the death of Eanmund, are recalled later in the poem at line 2659-2671.

2417 The Scylfings were a Swedish royal family whose name is used to refer to the Swedes, just as the Danes are called Scyldings because of the royal family's descent from Scyld Scefing.

2390 in the battle where Hygelac was killed,*
      when in the midst of the fight in Frisia
      the king of the Geats, Hrethel's son,
      lord and friend of the people, was drained
      by the thirsty sword, beaten by blade.
      Relying on his strength, Beowulf withdrew
      and swam away. As he made his way toward the sea
      he held in his arms the war-gear of thirty soldiers.
      Those who bore shields against him, the Hetwares,*
      had no reason to celebrate the fight on foot.
2400 After challenging that warrior, few returned
      to seek their homes. The son of Ecgtheow, alone
      and forlorn, swam over the sea's expanse
      back to his people. There Hygd offered him
      treasure and the kingdom, rings and the throne.
      Now that Hygelac was dead, his queen
      did not trust that her son knew how to guard
      the ancestral throne against a foreign army.
      But the desperate people could not in any way
      convince that thane that he should be
2410 lord over Heardred, nor did he wish
      to take the royal power. However,
      through friendly counsel, Beowulf advised
      Heardred with good will and kindness
      until he matured and could rule the Weather-Geats.

      Outcasts, sons of Ohthere, sought him out
      from across the sea.* They had rebelled
      against the protector of the Scylfings,*
      the best of sea-kings, the famous lord
      who dispensed treasures in Sweden.
2420 There he met his mortal end.
      In return for his hospitality, the son of Hygelac
      received a fatal wound from the stroke of a sword.
      After Heardred was killed, Onela,

2430 Although Onela allowed Beowulf to become king of the Geats, Beowulf helps Eadgils, Onela's nephew, attempt to seize the Swedish throne once again. This time Eadgils succeeds in becoming the king of the Swedes.

2433 The language is ambiguous as to whether the poem credits Beowulf or Eadgils for defeating Onela. These lines appear in a passage that seems to focus on the military exploits of Beowulf, but Scandinavian sagas make no mention of Beowulf when they describe how Eadgils (named Aðils in these sources) wins the throne. As Richard North has suggested, the phrase *gewræc...cealdum cearsiðum*, which we have rendered "sought cold vengeance," puns on Beowulf or Eadgils' state of mind and the fact that the sagas claim that this battle was fought on the ice of the frozen Lake Väner.

son of Ongentheow, departed from that land
to seek his home. He allowed Beowulf
to rule over the Geats, to guard the royal throne.
That was a good king.

XXXIV.
In later days, Beowulf resolved to avenge
the defeat of his people. He was a friend
2430   to Eadgils* in his time of desperation.
With warriors and weapons, he supported
the son of Ohthere across the wide sea.
He sought cold vengeance*
and deprived the king of his life.
Thus, the son of Ecgtheow had survived
each assault, each fierce battle, each valiant deed
until the day he had to fight the dragon.
The enraged Geatish king, as one of twelve men,
went to find the winged beast. He had learned
2440   how the feud arose, the acts of terror
inflicted on his men. Beowulf had received
the precious cup from the hand of the thief.
In that troop he was the thirteenth man,
the robber who provoked the conflict,
sad in mind. From there, humiliated,
he had to guide them to that place.
Against his will, he approached the earth-hall.
He knew the way to that barrow under the earth
near the turbulent waters of the surging sea.
2450   Inside, it was filled with finely patterned treasure.
The monstrous guardian, the ready fighter
protected its golden treasure, ancient under the earth.
That prize could not easily be won.
The battle-brave king sat down on the cliff,
the gold-friend of the Geats wished
his hearth-comrades luck. His troubled spirit

2473 The Old English here uses litotes once again, as Beowulf claims, "*Næs ic him to life / laðra owihte*" ("I was never more hateful to him than any of his sons"). This statement highlights Hrethel's affection for Beowulf and sets up the tragic story that Beowulf is about to recount in which one of Hrethel's sons, Hæthcyn, accidentally kills another son, Herebeald.

2474 The story of Hæthcyn and Herebeald appears to be based on an episode from Norse mythology in which the Norse god Hoðr accidentally kills his brother Baldr with an arrow. Commonality in name-elements (Baldr / -*beald*) and (Hoðr / *Hæth*-) emphasizes the parallels between the two accounts. The correspondence links Hrethel to the Norse god Oðinn, the father of both Baldr and Hoðr.

2481 Because Hæthcyn's death was caused by a member of his own family, the family cannot seek vengeance, nor will anyone pay or receive a *wergild*.

was restless and eager for slaughter.
The old man's fate was nearing, approaching,
seeking out the treasure of his soul, severing life
2460 from body. Not for long would the spirit
of the nobleman be enveloped in flesh.

Beowulf, son of Ecgtheow, spoke:
"In youth, I survived many battle-storms
in times of war. I remember everything.
I was seven winters old when
the lord of treasures, dear friend to our people,
received me from my father.
King Hrethel kept and sheltered me,
honored me with treasure and feasts,
2470 remembering our ties of kinship.
As a warrior in his strongholds,
his love for me was never less
than that for any of his sons,*
Herebeald and Hæthcyn or my Hygelac.*
Too soon, a death-bed was prepared
for the eldest son by the deed of his kinsman
after Hæthcyn struck his lord and friend
with an arrow from his horn-bow.
He missed the mark, shot his older brother dead,
2480 one son's blood on the other son's arrow.
There could be no compensation for this loss,*
a violent mistake leaving Hæthcyn heartsick.
Still, the unavenged nobleman had lost his life.

And so it is sad for an old man to endure
his young son swaying on the gallows.
He may recount a tale, a mournful song,
when his son hangs as a joy to the raven,
and he, though old and wise, cannot help him
or do anything. With each morning

2502 The poem says that the father sings songs of lamentation *an æfter anum*. This phrase suggests both that the father is singing one song after another and that the father is singing alone after one of his beloved sons has died.

2490	the death of his child comes to his mind.
	He has no interest in living
	to see another heir inside that stronghold,
	when one son, now claimed by death,
	has reached the end of his deeds.
	Sorrowful, he sees his son's private chamber
	in the deserted wine-hall, the windy resting-place
	deprived of music. The rider sleeps in death,
	the hero in his grave. The sound of the harp
	has faded. There is no joy in this home
2500	as there once was.

	XXXV.
	He goes to his bed and sings out songs of sorrow,
	one after another.* To him all seems
	too spacious, the fields and dwelling-place.
	Thus the lord of the Geats bore grief
	in his heart, stirred for Herebeald;
	in no way could he settle the feud
	with the slayer. He could not show hatred
	to that warrior through vengeful acts,
	though he did not love him.
2510	With the sorrow that befell him,
	he gave up the joy of men, chose God's light.
	When he departed from life, he left to his sons
	his land and estate, as a fortunate man does.
	Then there was hostility and conflict between
	the Swedes and Geats across the wide water.
	There was mutual anger and intense strife
	after Hrethel died. Ongentheow's sons,
	the Swedes, were war-minded and bold.
	They would not have friendship across the seas
2520	but instead would advance murderous attacks
	near Sorrow Hill. My dear kinsmen avenged
	that feud and violence, as was well known,

2528 Eofor is a Geatish warrior whose name means "boar." More details about this battle and Eofor's slaying of Ongentheow will be given in lines 2970-3070.

2537 The Gepids were a Germanic tribe that occupied parts of southern Sweden.

2546 Dæghrefn means "Day-Raven". He is identified in the poem as a *Huga cempan* ("champion of the Hugas"). Some critics believe Hugas to be another name for the Franks, but others assume that the Hugas were Frisian.

2548 Some readers have wondered whether the *breostweorðung* ("breast-ornament" or "neck-ring") that Beowulf takes from Dæghrefn is the same neck-ring that Wealhtheow had given to Beowulf. Hygelac was wearing that neck-ring when he fell in battle, as we learned in line 1190. If Dæghrefn killed Hygelac, as most critics believe the poem implies, then he may have stripped the Geatish king of the neck-ring so that he could wear it as a trophy.

although the elder paid with his life,
a hard bargain. That war was fatal to Hæthcyn,
the Geatish lord. I have heard that
in the morning the other kinsman, Hygelac,
sought vengeance for Hæthcyn in battle.
Ongentheow pursued Eofor* but the old Swede fell,
his color drained by the sword, his battle-helmet
2530   split open. Eofor's hand recalled many feuds;
it did not hold back the mortal blow.

For the treasures Hygelac had given me,
I repaid him with my service in battle
as fate granted, using my gleaming sword.
He gave me a domain, the joy of a homeland.
There was no need for him to seek
from among the Gepids* or the Spear-Danes
or the Swedes a less worthy warrior to hire.
I always wished to be in front of him
2540   in the foot-troop, at the head of the vanguard.
And so I shall fight battles all my life,
as long as this sword endures, the blade
that has stood by me in the past
and will continue to do so, ever since,
in front of the proven warriors,
I became the slayer of Dæghrefn,*
the Huga champion, with my bare hands.
He could not bring treasure or his neck-ring*
to the Frisian king, but in combat he fell,
2550   this standard bearer, valorous nobleman.
The sword was not his slayer, but my battle-grip
crushed his bone-house, his throbbing heart.
Now the edge of the sword, the hand,
and the bold blade must clash over the hoard."

Beowulf spoke, making his last boast:

"I braved many battles in my youth,
yet I, old guardian of the people,
will seek out that feud, will perform
a glorious deed if the scourge of men
2560   seeks me out from its earth-hall."
He greeted every man, the bold warriors,
his own dear comrades, for the last time:
"I would not bear a sword against the dragon
if I knew how to nobly engage my adversary
as I did before, grappling with Grendel,
but there I expect deadly fire, hot breath
and venom, so I am armed with a shield
and mail-coat. I do not wish to move
even a foot from the barrow guardian,
2570   but it must unfold between us at the mound,
as fate, the ruler of every man, decides.
I am so bold at heart that I will forgo
boasting before the winged attacker.
Wait here on the barrow, protected
by mail-coats, men in war-gear,
to see which of us can better survive
his wounds after the bloody encounter.
It is not your duty, nor is it in the power
of any man except me alone,
2580   to fight against my adversary's strength,
to perform heroic deeds. With courage,
I will win gold unless perilous battle,
deadly evil, carries off your lord."

The brave warrior stood beside his shield,
sturdy under his helmet. He bore
his coat of mail beneath the rocky cliffs,
confident in his own strength.
This was no coward's task.
The valiant warrior who had survived

2590   many wars, many battles when troops collided,
        saw a stone arch standing along the wall.
        Through there a stream burst out of the barrow,
        the surge of that current hot with deadly fire.
        He could not approach the treasure,
        nor could he remain in the hollow passage
        for any length of time unburnt by dragon-flame.
        Enraged, Beowulf unleashed a word
        from his breast; the stout-hearted one shouted.
        His voice rang clear in battle, echoing
2600   under the gray stone. Hatred erupted;
        the dragon recognized the voice of a man.
        There was no time to seek friendship.
        First from the cavern came the enemy's breath,
        burning vapor. The ground shook.
        In the barrow, the warrior, lord of the Geats,
        swung his shield against the grim beast.
        The heart of the dragon was roused to fight.
        The good war-king had already drawn his sword,
        an ancient heirloom, its edge no longer bright.
2610   Each one inspired terror in the other.
        The steadfast warrior held his position,
        bracing himself behind his high shield.
        The dragon quickly coiled; Beowulf tensed
        in his war-gear. The smoldering dragon slithered
        and slinked, hastening toward its fate.
        The shield protected life and body
        for less time than the famous lord had hoped.
        There, at that moment, he had to perform
        for the first time without fate granting him
2620   triumph in battle.The lord of the Geats
        raised his hand and struck the glistering creature
        with his mighty weapon; blunt on the bone,
        the edge failed. It bit less strongly than
        the king had needed, hard-pressed by the foe.

2650 It is unclear whether this identification of Wiglaf's father as *leod Scylfinga* ("man of the Scylfings") implies that he is Swedish by birth or through his allegiance to the Swedish king Onela.

2654 The Wægmundings are the clan and family to which Beowulf and Wiglaf belong. There is some debate as to the origins of the Wægmundings, for some contend they are both Swedish and Geatish while others insist they are fully Geatish, like the Hrethlings. The Swedish theory is supported both by the contention that Ecgtheow (Beowulf's father) was Swedish and by the Swedish loyalties of Weohstan (Wiglaf's father).

After the sword-blow, the barrow's guardian
was incensed; it expelled murderous fire.
Flames billowed all around.
Beowulf did not boast of victory.
The bare blade had failed in battle
2630   as it never should have,
that iron sword, once so good.
In no way was that an easy undertaking,
when the renowned son of Ecgtheow
was forced to give up ground.
Against his will he stepped back,
just as each man must let go of his transitory days.
Soon, the enemies faced each other again.
The guardian of the hoard took heart,
its breast surging with new breath.
2640   Beowulf narrowly persisted, surrounded by fire,
he who had once ruled the people.
None of the comrades in his troop, no sons of noblemen,
stood by him with honor, but instead they fled
into the wood to preserve their lives.
Among them one spirit surged with sorrow.
Nothing could turn aside the ties of kinship
for he who thinks rightly.

XXXVI.
He was called Wiglaf,
Weohstan's son, the dear shield-warrior,
2650   man of the Scylfings,* Ælfher's kinsman.
He saw his liege lord suffering the heat
under his war-mask. He remembered then
the benefits that he had been given,
the grand dwelling place of Wægmundings,*
all the property his father had inherited.
He could not hold himself back.

2660 Eanmund, son of Ohthere and brother of Eadgils, was previously discussed at line 2383. Here we learn that it was Weohstan, Wiglaf's father, who slew Eanmund during the Swedish attack on the Geats. Eanmund's sword has now been passed down to Wiglaf. Eadgils, who had seized the Swedish throne with the help of Beowulf (lines 2429-2434), would need to attack the Geats and kill Wiglaf in order to avenge the death of his brother.

His hand seized the yellow lindenwood shield,
and he drew his ancient sword.
It was known among the ancestors
2660   to be the heirloom of Eanmund, Ohthere's son.*
Weohstan slew that friendless exile
in battle with the sword's edge
and carried to his kinsmen the shining helmet,
the mail-coat formed of rings,
and the ancient sword made by giants.
Onela granted Weohstan his nephew's war-gear,
ready armor. Onela never spoke about the feud,
though Weohstan killed his brother's son.
Weohstan kept the treasures for many seasons,
2670   blade and coat of mail, until his own son,
Wiglaf, would assume the title of his father.
He gave him then, now living among the Geats,
a wealth of war-equipment when he departed
from this life, old and wise in his journey forth.

Now was the first time the young warrior
had to perform with his dear lord in battle.
His spirit did not melt, nor did his kinsman's
sword fail, as the dragon discovered after
they faced each other. Wiglaf made a speech
2680   reminding the retainers of their duty.
His mind was mournful: "I remember
the time when we shared mead in the hall,
when we promised our lord who gave us
these rings that we would repay him
by wielding war-equipment, helmets
and strong swords, if difficulty should befall him.
He personally chose us from the ranks
for this expedition. He considered us
deserving of fame, and he gave me these gifts.
2690   He deemed us worthy spearmen

2721 The Old English phrase *fyrwylmum fah fionda niosian* is ambiguous. The word *fah* functions here as a substantive adjective meaning either "hostile" or "decorated" and the dative *fyrwylmum* can modify either *fah* or *niosian* ("sought" or "attacked"). It could be read, therefore, as either "the [one] decorated with fire-surges sought/attacked his enemies" or "the hostile [one] sought/attacked his enemies with fire-surges."

and bold warriors, though our lord intended
to perform his valiant feat alone. For men
he has done the most glorious deeds,
the most reckless deeds.
Now the day has come that our liege lord
needs strength in good warriors;
let us go forth to help the war-leader,
as long as the grim flames threaten.
God knows that I would rather be together
2700   with my beloved gold-giver in the fire's embrace,
for it does not seem proper to me
that we carry our shields back to the homeland
unless we first cut down the enemy
and protect the life of our king.
I know his past deeds were not of so little value
that out of all the proven Geatish warriors,
he alone should suffer this affliction,
fall in the fight. The sword and helmet,
the mail-coat and corslet must be shared among us."

2710   Wiglaf made his way through the deadly fumes,
bearing his helmet to the king in support,
and spoke a few words: "Beloved Beowulf,
you must succeed. When you were young
you said that for as long as you lived,
you would never let your glory fade;
now, brave and determined lord, you must
fight for your life with valiant deeds
and all of your strength. I will help you."
After those words, the furious serpent
2720   attacked again. Gleaming with surges of fire,
the terrible foe sought out his enemies,*
the hated men. The fire shot forth
in waves, the shield burned to its center.
The young warrior's mail-coat

2732 This is the first time that Beowulf's sword is named. Nægling means "nailer." Erin Mullally suggests that Nægling is Hrethel's sword, which Hygelac had presented to Beowulf in line 2215, but the poem never makes that explicit. Beowulf's sword is reminiscent of Nagelring, a supposedly unbreakable sword in the *Vilkina Saga*.

2738 *Klaeber 4* notes that there are a number of heroes in Germanic and Norse literature whose strength is so great that their swords break when they wield them.

could not protect him, so with courage
he ducked behind his kinsman's shield,
since his own was destroyed by flames.
The war-king called to mind his glorious deeds.
With tremendous strength, driven by fury,
2730   he struck the dragon so that
the battle-sword lodged in its head.
Nægling snapped.*
Beowulf's sword, ancient and gray,
failed him. It was not granted by fate
that iron swords could help him in battle;
his hand was too strong. I have heard
that he overstressed each blade
with his sword-stroke.* When he brought
to battle a weapon tempered by blood,
2740   it did him no good. The people's foe,
the perilous fire-serpent, seethed with rage.
For a third time it rushed at the brave man
when opportunity allowed. Hot and battle-grim,
it clasped his neck with sharp fangs.
He became drenched with life-blood;
the crimson gushed in waves.

XXXVII.
I have heard that when the king was in need,
the nobleman beside him showed courage,
power, and bravery, as was in his nature.
2750   Wiglaf failed to heed the dragon's head,
so the hand of the courageous man
was burned when he helped his kinsman.
Aiming slightly lower, the retainer
in his armor struck the vile creature.
The shiny, gold-plated sword plunged
into its body, and the fire began to subside.
Then the king collected his wits.

He drew a dagger, bitter and battle-sharp,
that he carried in his mail-coat.
2760 The protector of the Geats sliced
across the dragon's underbelly.
They cut down the enemy
– their courage extinguished its life –
and both killed it, those noble kinsmen.
A man ought to behave in such a way
when a thane is in need. For the king
that was the last victory by his own deeds,
his final worldly work. The wound
the dragon had given him began to burn
2770 and swell. He realized that a grave affliction
welled in his breast, venom within.
The lord walked to the wall
and sank onto a stone slab.
He looked at the giant-work, noticed
how the stone arches and fixed pillars
supported the age-old earth-hall from within.
With his hands, the exceptional retainer
washed his famed lord with water,
his bloodstained king wearied by war,
2780 and unfastened his helmet. Beowulf spoke
through the pain, the searing wound.
He knew well that he had completed
his days of earthly joy, his life-span
finished, death all too near:
"Now I would have given war-gear
to my son, if fate had granted that an heir,
related by blood, would follow after me.
For fifty winters I ruled these people;
no king of any neighboring nation dared
2790 attack me with swords or threaten me with violence.
In my homeland I awaited my destined end,
protected my realm. I did not seek out hostilities,

2821 The word *oferhigian*, rendered here as "triumph," presents a problem for translators since this is the only appearance of this Old English compound in Anglo-Saxon literature. We agree with *Klaeber 4* that the word should be read as "over-strive" or "over-take," meaning that the treasure will always outlast the efforts of any one man or group to control it.

nor falsely swear oaths. Though now stricken
with mortal wounds, I find joy in all these things.
The Lord need not accuse me of the slaughter
of kinsmen when life departs from my body.
Go quickly, dear Wiglaf, to survey the hoard
under the gray stones, now that the dragon
lies asleep in death, grievously wounded,
2800   bereft of his treasure. Make haste,
so that I may behold the ancient wealth,
the golden riches, and look upon the bright,
precious gems. I will then be able, in light
of this hoard, to more easily give up my life
and the nation that I have long held."

XXXVIII.
I have heard that Wiglaf swiftly obeyed
the words of the wounded lord, sick
from battle. Wearing a woven mail-coat
the retainer moved quickly under the roof
2810   of the dragon's barrow. The victorious one,
the brave man, saw many precious jewels
when he walked by Beowulf's seat,
glittering gold lying on the ground,
wonders on the walls in this lair
of the dragon, the ancient night-flyer,
goblets made for men in older days, scattered,
unpolished, their adornments lost.
There were many time-worn helmets
and tarnished arm-rings, skillfully twisted.
2820   Treasure, gold in the earth, will always
triumph, however well a man may hide it.*
He also saw a gold-threaded standard
displayed over the treasure, the greatest
of hand-made marvels, interlaced with fine skill.
A light emanated from the banner, allowing him

2851 Editors believe a half-line to be missing, and *Biorncyning spræc* ("the king of men spoke") or *Bregorof gespræc* ("the majestic one spoke") have been offered as emendations.

2859 In the phrase *fremmað gena / leoda þearfe*, the verb *fremmað* has been understood as either a plural imperative or a plural indicative with a future sense. Therefore, it might read "use these [treasures] to support the needs of my people" or "these [treasures] will support the needs of my people." Alfred Bammesberger suggests that the plural *fremmað* uses an implied "they" to refer to his men (identified as *heaðomære* a few lines down). In this case, the phrase would read "the battle-famed men will use these treasures..."

      The use of the plural seems odd since Beowulf is addressing only Wiglaf. We agree with Robert Bjork's argument in "Speech as Gift in *Beowulf*" that the inappropriate use of the plural form contributes to the irony of Beowulf's final words.

to survey the floor, examine the treasures.
There was no sign of the dragon,
for the swordblade destroyed it.
I have heard that Wiglaf, alone,
2830 plundered the treasure in the burial mound,
the ancient handiwork of giants.
He filled his arms with goblets and dishes
of his own choosing; he also seized
the standard, the brightest of beacons.
The sword of the old king, its iron edge,
had harmed the guardian of the treasure
who had long defended its hoard
with terrible flames, waging destruction
in the middle of the night, until it was slain.
2840 Then Wiglaf went in haste, eager to return,
spurred by the treasure. He was anxious
to know whether he would find
the bold-hearted man alive in that place,
the prince of the Geats, failing in strength,
there where he had left him. Wiglaf,
carrying the treasure, found the illustrious king,
the bloody lord at the end of his life.
He began to splash Beowulf with water
until the first of his words broke through his breast-hoard.
2850 The old man examined the gold in sorrow.
[Beowulf spoke]*: "With these words
I offer thanks to the Lord of all,
to the King of glory, to the eternal Prince,
for this treasure I now gaze upon,
which I was allowed to acquire
for my men before my death-day.
Now that I have paid for the treasures
of the hoard with my old life, use them
to support the needs of my people.*
2860 I may not be here much longer.

2861 The verb *hatað* ("command") presents the same problem as *fremmað*, as discussed above in the note for 2859. Beowulf is either asking Wiglaf to order the construction of a burial mound, or he is predicting that his men will command that one be built.

2869 This might be the necklace originally given to Beowulf by Wealhtheow and recovered by Beowulf when he slew Dæghrefn (line 2546).

XXIX The manuscript indicates the start of a new fitt with a capital letter, but there is no corresponding Roman numeral.

2889 "Leavings of hammers" (*homera lafe*) is another way to refer to a sword. In the process of making a sword, iron blades were heated in furnaces before being pounded into shape. Thus, the sword is what remains when the excess metal has been hammered away.

Command* battle-famed men to build
a splendid burial mound at the edge of the sea
after my funeral pyre burns. It must be
to my people a memorial, a high tower
on Whale's Cape so that seafarers
in years to come might call it
the Barrow of Beowulf, when tall ships
ride from afar over the dark water."
The stout-hearted king removed his golden neck-ring*
2870 and gave it to the young retainer, along with
his gold-plated helmet, jeweled ring, and corslet.
He ordered Wiglaf to make good use of them:
"You are the last remnant of our kin,
the last of the Wægmundings.
Fate has swept all of my kinsmen
to their destined end, valiant warriors.
I shall follow after them."
                              This was the last word
from the old man's heart-thoughts before he chose
the funeral pyre, hot with surging flames.
2880 His soul went from his breast to seek
the judgment of the righteous.

[XXXIX.]*
It pained the young man to see
his beloved lord on the ground,
his life at an end, suffering terribly.
The murderer also lay dead, the awful
earth-dragon deprived of life.
The coiled serpent could no longer
guard the ring-hoard; the battle-notched,
hard iron edges, leavings of hammers,*
2890 had destroyed it. The far-flier, stilled
by its wounds, had fallen to the ground
near the treasure-cave. Never again

would it fly at midnight, exult in the bright
presence of treasure, for it fell to the earth,
a victim of the warrior's handiwork.
Indeed, as I have heard, there was seldom
a man among the mighty ones in this world
who has so greatly prospered, however daring
he was in every exploit, charging
2900 against the breath of a venomous rival
or disturbing the ring-hall with his hands,
even if he discovered that the guardian
who lived in the barrow was watching.
Beowulf was rewarded in death
with a portion of lordly treasure.
Each foe had reached the end of a fleeting life.

A short time later, the oath-breaking
cowards, ten altogether, left the woods,
after they had not dared to wield spears
2910 when their liege lord was in dire need.
Ashamed, they bore their shields and armor
to the place where the aged king lay.
They gazed at Wiglaf. The weary retainer
sat close by the shoulder of his lord,
trying to wake him with water.
He did not succeed.
As much as he wished, he could not
save the life of his lord, nor change
anything that was God's will. The judgment
2920 of God would rule the action of every man,
as it still does. An angry rebuke
from the young man was readily given
to those who had lost their valor.
Wiglaf, son of Weohstan, sad at heart,
looked upon those unloved men and spoke:
"It may be said by one who speaks truth

that this lord gave you many precious treasures
and the battle-dress in which you now stand.
He often distributed helmets and coats of mail
2930   to his men on the mead-benches,
gifts from the king to his followers,
the finest treasures that he could find,
far or near. It now seems as though
he was rashly throwing away battle-gear
when war came to him. The king had no reason
to boast about his comrades, but God,
the Lord of Victory, granted that Beowulf,
alone with his sword, could seek vengeance
when he was in need of courage.
2940   I could provide little life-protection in battle;
nevertheless, I acted beyond my measure
to help my kinsman. The dragon grew weaker
when I struck it with my sword,
the deadly foe, the fire from its mouth
subsiding. Too few rallied around the king
when peril arose. Now, the awarding of treasure
and the giving of swords, all your joys
and all you hold dear shall come to an end.
Each man will lose land-rights
2950   in his nation, after foreign noblemen
learn of your flight, your infamous act.
For warriors, death is better than a life of shame."

XL.
Wiglaf ordered that the outcome of the battle
be announced at the encampment atop the cliff
by the water's edge where a band of retainers,
heart-sad shield-bearers, sat through the long morning.
They expected either the death or the return
of their beloved leader. Wiglaf's messenger
was not silent when he rode up with new tidings,

2981 The Merovingians were the ruling dynasty of the Franks until 751 when the Merovingian line was succeeded by the Carolingians. Charlemagne, the founder of the Holy Roman Empire, descended from the Carolingian line.

2960   speaking truly to all: "Now the lord
and benefactor of the Geats is bound
to his deathbed by the dragon's deeds.
The vicious foe lies dead beside him,
stricken with stab wounds. Beowulf
could not find a way to inflict a wound
on the cruel enemy with his sword.
Wiglaf, son of Weohstan, sits with Beowulf.
Heart-weary, the warrior guards the bodies,
watching over both the loved and the loathed.

2970   Now it is clear that we should expect war,
a battle against Frisians and Franks,
once the fall of the king is made known
far and wide. Intense animosity arose
among the Franks after Hygelac traveled
into Frisian land with a fleet of ships.
There the Frankish tribe attacked,
fighting with courage and superior force
until the mailed warrior was killed in battle,
fallen among his troops. The leader would not

2980   be giving treasure to his men. After that,
the good will of the Merovingians*
was always denied to us. I have no reason
to expect peace or good faith from the Swedes,
since it was widely known that Ongentheow
deprived Hæthcyn, son of Hrethel, of his life
near Ravenswood when the men of the Geats,
out of pride, first attacked the War-Scylfings.
Without hesitation, the old father of Ohthere,
ancient and terrible, retaliated. He killed

2990   the sea-king and rescued his wife,
Onela and Ohthere's mother, an old woman
deprived of her gold, then pursued his deadly foes
until they barely escaped into Ravenswood,
leaderless. Ohthere, with his army,

3017 Protective walls erected around forts, castles, and towns were sometimes made using wood and dirt.

3024 The name Wulf means "wolf." Wonred means "unreasonable."

then besieged the wound-weary few
who had evaded the swords. He threatened
the miserable company throughout the night,
announced his intention to kill them
in the morning, some with the swordblade,
3000   some on the gallows-tree, sport for the birds.
Comfort came to the sad-hearted men at dawn
when they heard the sound of Hygelac's horn
and trumpet, when the good man arrived
with proven warriors following behind.

XLI.

The bloody track of the Swedes and Geats,
the brutal slaughter of men, was visible
far and wide, how the people among them
stirred a feud. Then the good and noble
Ongentheow, old and forlorn, departed
3010   with his kinsmen to seek the stronghold,
to move to higher ground. Because he had heard
of Hygelac's might, proud skill in battle,
Ongentheow did not trust in his ability
to repel their attack, nor to withstand
the seafarers so he might protect treasure,
sons, and wives. Afterwards, the old man fled
from there to the earth-wall.* Then the order
was given to pursue the Swedes.
Hygelac's banners advanced across the field
3020   after the sons of Hrethel swarmed the camp.
There, gray-haired Ongentheow was forced
by the swordblade to surrender; the king
had to submit to the judgment of Eofor alone.
Wulf, son of Wonred,* angrily struck him
with a weapon, his swing causing blood
to gush from the veins on his brow.
However, he was not afraid, the old Scylfing,

but quickly repaid him with a worse
counter-stroke, a deadly blow when the king
3030   turned to face him. Wulf, the brave
son of Wonred, could not give his own
counter-stroke to the old man, for Ongentheow
had cut through the helmet on Wulf's head
so that he, stained with blood, should have fallen
in battle. Wulf sank to the earth but was not
doomed to die. His wound gaped,
but he recovered nevertheless.
As his brother lay on the ground, Eofor,
Hygelac's brave retainer, with his broad
3040   sword, immense and ancient, broke through
the shield-wall and smashed the helmet
made by giants. The king fell,
keeper of his people. Ongentheow's life
was taken. Many helped to bandage Wulf,
their kinsman, and they quickly raised him up
once they were able to control the battlefield.
One warrior plundered Ongentheow.
He took from him his iron corslet,
hard, hilted sword, and also his helmet,
3050   and brought the adornments of the aged one
to Hygelac. He accepted those treasures
and, before his people, courteously promised
to reward them and to stand by that oath.
When he came home, the lord of the Geats,
the son of Hrethel, repaid Eofor and Wulf
for their battle-work with excessive treasure.
He gave each man a tremendous amount
of land and twisted rings – no man on earth
could reproach him for that reward
3060   after winning those war-glories –
he also gave to Eofor his only daughter
and the pride of his home, a pledge of favor.

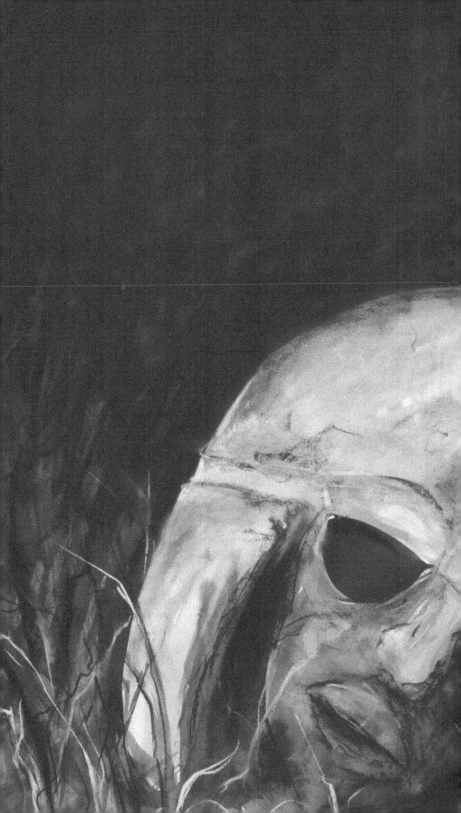

This is the feud, the deadly enmity,
for which I expect the men of the Swedes
will attack us after they learn that our king
is lifeless, he who had protected the hoard
and kingdom from foes after the fall
of the valiant Scylfing heroes, he who had
supported the people's welfare, and,
3070   beyond that, performed heroic deeds.
Now it is best to hurry to the hoard
so that we might look upon the king
and bring our ring-giver to the funeral pyre.
More than a mere portion of the treasure
should burn with that courageous man.
There is a hoard, countless gold
grimly bought, and now those rings
have been paid for with the end of his life.
Fire will devour, flames will engulf.
3080   No man will wear the treasure as remembrance,
nor will any beautiful woman keep
a ring adornment around her neck,
but, deprived of gold, those sad at heart
must roam foreign lands now that our leader
has given up laughter, revelry, and mirth.
Therefore, many a morning-cold spear
must be grasped in hand and hefted.
The music of the harp will fail
to awaken the warriors, but the dark raven,
3090   eager above the dead, will speak, telling
the eagle how he thrived at the meal
and, alongside the wolf, plundered the slain."

Thus the messenger declared terrible tidings.
Neither his predictions nor his words
were spoken falsely. The entire company rose,
went without joy under Eagle's Cliff

to behold the wonder with welling tears.
They found the lifeless king on the sand
guarding his bed of rest, the one
3100 who had given them rings in earlier times.
His final day had come to pass, the war-king,
the lord of the Geats, died a remarkable death.
First, they had seen the strange creature,
the dragon on the plain opposite
where his enemy lay dead: that fire-dragon,
fiercely and horribly gleaming, scorched
by its own flames. It lay fifty feet long on the ground.
It had ruled the joyous nighttime air
and afterwards went down to seek its den,
3110 but now it was firm in death, its use
of the earth-cave was at an end.
Its goblets and vessels stood beside it,
dishes and precious swords, rusted
and eaten through, as if they had lain
in the bosom of the earth for a thousand winters.
This inheritance, the gold of bygone men,
had been bound by a spell, so that no man
was able to reach the ring-hall unless
God himself, the true king of victory,
3120 – He is the protector of men –
allowed whomever He willed to open the hoard,
whichever man seemed fitting to Him.

XLII.
It was clear that the one who wrongfully hid
treasure inside those walls did not profit
from his labor. The guardian killed
that exceptional man, and then the feud
was settled, cruelly avenged.
It is a wonder as to where a brave warrior
might reach the end of his life,

3139 The Old English reads *Næs he goldhwæte, gearwor hæfde / agendes est ær gesceawod.* While the poem describes a curse on the gold, syntactic and lexical ambiguities have led scholars and translators to debate the implications of this curse for Beowulf. Some have argued that Beowulf will be damned by the curse because he sought the gold out of personal greed. Others suggest Beowulf is exempt from the curse because he sacrificed his life for the greater good of his people. In *Heroic Identity in the World of Beowulf*, Scott Gwara surveys the critical approaches to this passage and ultimately renders these lines as "not at all had he ever before looked more intently at his own gold-luck, an owner's generosity," which suggests that Beowulf merely "examined the dragon's cache more closely than any other gift he had ever received, an act of studied appraisal" (pp. 280-85). Because of the debate regarding this passage, we have done our best to render the literal sense, leaving our reader to judge whether Beowulf will escape the curse placed on the hoard or whether these lines should be read ironically.

3130   when this man can no longer reside
in the mead-hall with his kinsmen;
so it was for Beowulf when he sought
the guardian of the barrow in battle.
He could not have known
how he would depart from this world.
The glorious kings, those who had buried
the gold, had solemnly declared that,
until Judgment Day, the men who plundered
the hoard would be guilty of wrongdoing,
3140   confined to heathen temples, fixed
in the bonds of hell, tormented by affliction.
In no way was Beowulf cursed by the gold-spell
as he gazed upon the owner's generosity.*

Wiglaf, son of Weohstan, spoke:
"Often, because of the will of one,
many will endure misery, as has happened for us.
We could not, with any counsel,
persuade the king, keeper of the realm,
not to attack the guardian of gold and instead
3150   to let it lie where it had long resided,
remain in its home until the world's end.
He fulfilled his high destiny.
The hoard is uncovered but was won
at a hard price. The fate was too strong
that drove Beowulf there. After the path
was cleared, I ventured inside and saw
the treasure, but it was no easy feat
to make my way inside the earth-walls.
In haste, I gathered a great heap of treasure
3160   from the hoard and carried it back to my king.
He was then still alive, conscious and sound of mind.
He said a great many things, the old man in sorrow,
and he ordered me to greet you. He asked that you,

in memory of his deeds, build a mound
for a funeral pyre, towering and brilliant,
for he was the best of warriors far and wide,
throughout the earth, for as long as he enjoyed
the wealth of the royal stronghold.
Let us hurry once again to seek and see
3170   the pile of precious gems, wonders
beneath the earth. I will lead you,
so that you may closely examine
many rings and abounding gold.
Swiftly, have the funeral bier prepared
before we come out, that we might carry
our king, the beloved man, to where he
shall long remain in the Lord's keeping."

Wiglaf, the dauntless man, commanded noblemen
to bring funeral wood for the great war-leader:
3180   "Now shall fire devour him, the dark flame
bathe the lord of warriors who often endured
the iron-shower when storms of arrows
afflicted him, flying over the shield-wall,
the shafts performing their duty,
primed feathers aided by arrowheads."
Indeed, the wise son of Weohstan
summoned the best retainers from the troop,
seven altogether. He, one of eight warriors,
walked beneath the barrow's wicked roof;
3190   the man in front carried a torch in his hand.
They did not cast lots to decide who would plunder
that hoard, since, without a guardian,
any portion that yet remained for the men
was only temporary. They felt little remorse
for removing the noble treasure. They pushed
the dragon, guardian of the hoard, over the cliff,
let it be taken by the waves, the flood's embrace.

Then twisted gold was loaded on a wagon,
a huge amount of treasure, and the king,
3200   the aged warrior, was brought to Whale's Cape.

XLIII.
For him the men of the Geats prepared
a magnificent funeral pyre on the earth,
adorned with helmets, war-shields,
and shining mail-coats as he had requested.
They laid their renowned king in the center,
men mourning their beloved lord.
On the cliff they began to kindle
the greatest of funeral pyres.
Dark wood-smoke ascended, black over fire,
3210   the flames' roar woven with wailing
–the swirling wind subsided–
until the blaze had broken his bone-house,
hot in the core. Sad at heart, the people
gave voice to their grief, bemoaned
their liege lord's death. A Geatish woman,
her hair bound up, sang an elegy
for the death of Beowulf, a sorrowful song.
Again and again she cried out
that she sorely dreaded the days of lamentation,
3220   the great number of violent deaths, the terrors
of her people, humiliation and captivity.
Heaven swallowed the smoke.
The people of the Geats assembled
a burial mound on the cliff, high and broad,
visible far and wide to seafarers.
It was constructed in ten days,
the beacon of the battle-strong.
They surrounded the leavings of the fire
with a wall as worthy as the wisest men
3230   could possibly devise. Into the barrow

they placed rings and jewels,
all such adornments, that had been taken
from the hoard by men who know strife.
They left the treasure of the princes
for the earth to guard, gold in the ground,
where it still remains, as useless to men
as it ever was. The brave sons of noblemen,
twelve in all, rode around the barrow.
They longed to wail with sorrow
3240   and mourn for the king, to deliver an elegy
and speak about the man, to praise his nobility
and admire his valiant deeds. Thus it is fitting
that a man praise his lord and friend
with words and love him with his heart
when he must be led forth from his body.
The people of the Geats, hearth-companions,
cried for the death of their lord:
they said that he was, of all the earthly kings,
the most generous and gracious to men,
3250   the kindest to his people and most eager for fame.

Works Cited, Consulted, and Recommended for Further Study

Editions and Translations

Chickering, Howell D., Jr. *Beowulf: A Dual-Language Edition.* New York: Anchor Books, 1977.

Heaney, Seamus. *Beowulf: A Verse Translation.* Ed. Daniel Donoghue. New York: W.W. Norton, 2006.

Klaeber's Beowulf. 4th edition. R.D. Fulk, Robert E. Bjork, and John D. Niles, eds. Toronto: University of Toronto Press, 2008.

Mitchell, Bruce and Fred C. Robinson, eds. *Beowulf: An Edition.* Oxford: Blackwell, 1998.

Sullivan, Alan and Timothy Murphy, trans. *Beowulf: A Longman Cultural Edition.* Ed. Sarah Anderson. New York: Pearson Longman, 2004.

Scholarship

A Beowulf Handbook. Robert E. Bjork and John D. Niles, eds. Lincoln: University of Nebraska Press, 1997.

Atherton, Mark. "The Figure of the Archer in *Beowulf* and the Anglo-Saxon Psalter." *Neophilologus* 77 (1993): 653-57.

Bammesberger, Alfred. "Beowulf's Last Will." *English Studies* 77 (1996): 305-10.

Biggs, Frederick M. "Hondscioh and Æschere in *Beowulf*." *Neophilologus* 87 (2003): 635-52.

———. "The Politics of Succession in *Beowulf* and Anglo-Saxon England." *Speculum* 80 (2005): 709-41.

Bjork, Robert E. "Speech as Gift in *Beowulf*." *Speculum* 69 (1994): 993-1022.

Campbell, James, Eric John, and Patrick Wormald. *The Anglo-Saxons*. New York: Penguin, 1991.

Chance, Jane. *Woman as Hero in Old English Literature*. Syracuse: Syracuse University Press, 1986.

Clemoes, Peter. *Interactions of Thought and Language in Old English Poetry*. Cambridge: Cambridge University Press, 1995.

Davidson, Hilda Ellis. *The Sword in Anglo-Saxon England*. Oxford: Clarendon Press, 1962.

Day, David D. "Hands Across the Hall: The Legalities of Beowulf's Fight with Grendel." *Journal of English and Germanic Philology* 98 (1999): 313-24.

Earl, James W. "*Beowulf* and the Origins of Civilization," in *The Postmodern Beowulf: A Critical Casebook*, 249-85. Eileen A. Joy and Mary K. Ramsey, eds. Morgantown: West Virginia University Press, 2006.

———. "Reading *Beowulf* with Original Eyes," in *The Postmodern Beowulf: A Critical Casebook*, 687-704. Eileen A Joy and Mary K. Ramsey, eds. Morgantown: West Virginia University Press, 2006.

Enright, Michael J. "The Warband Contexts of the Unferth Episode." *Speculum* 73 (1998): 297-337.

Fulk, Robert D. "Unferth and His Name." *Modern Philology* 85 (1987): 113-27.

———. "The Name of Offa's Queen: *Beowulf* 1931-2." *Anglia* 122 (2004): 614-39.

———. "Some Emendations and Non-Emendations in *Beowulf* (Verses 600a, 976a, 1585b, 1663b, 1740a, 2525b, 2771a, and 3060a)." *Studies in Philology* 104 (2007): 159-74.

Gahrn, Lars. "The Geats of *Beowulf*." *Scandinavian Journal of History* 11 (1986): 95-113.

Galloway, Andrew. "*Beowulf* and the Varieties of Choice." *PMLA* 105 (1990): 197-208.

Griffith, Mark S. "Some Difficulties in *Beowulf*, lines 874-902: Sigemund Reconsidered." *Anglo-Saxon England* 24 (1995): 11-41.

Gwara, Scott. *Heroic Identity in the World of Beowulf.* Leiden: Brill, 2008.

Hiatt, Alfred. "*Beowulf* Off the Map." *Anglo-Saxon England.* 38 (2009): 11-40.

Hill, John M. *The Cultural World in Beowulf.* Toronto: University of Toronto Press, 1995.

———. *The Anglo-Saxon Warrior Ethic: Reconstructing Lordship in Early English Literature.* Gainesville: University Press of Florida, 2000.

Howe, Nicholas. *Migration and Mythmaking in Anglo-Saxon England.* New Haven: Yale University Press, 1989.

Hughes, Geoffrey. "Beowulf, Unferth, and Hrunting: An Interpretation." *English Studies* 58 (1977): 385-95.

Hume, Kathryn. "The Function of the *Hrefn Blaca: Beowulf* 1801." *Modern Philology* 67 (1969): 60-3.

Juranski, Stefan. *Ancient Privileges: Beowulf, Law and the Making of Germanic Antiquity*. Morgantown: West Virginia University Press, 2006.

Kaske, Robert E. "The Sigemund-Heremod and Hama-Hygelac Passages in *Beowulf*." *PMLA* 74 (1959): 489-94.

———. "'Hygelac' and 'Hygd,'" in Studies in *Old English Literature in Honor of Arthur G. Brodeur*, 200-6. Ed. Stanley B. Greenfield. Eugene: University of Oregon Books, 1963.

———. "The *Eotenas* in *Beowulf*," in *Old English Poetry: Fifteen Essays*, 285-310. Ed. Robert P. Creed. Providence: Brown University Press, 1967.

Lapidge, Michael. "*Beowulf* and the Psychology of Terror," in *Heroic Poetry in the Anglo-Saxon Period, Studies in Honor of Jess B. Bessinger, Jr.*, 373-402. Helen Damico and John Leyrele, eds. Kalamazoo: Medieval Institute Publications, 1993.

Lerer, Seth. "Grendel's Glove." *ELH* 61 (1994): 721-51.

Leyerle, John. "The Interlace Structure of *Beowulf*." *University of Toronto Quarterly* 37 (1967): 1-17.

Malone, Kemp. "Notes on *Beowulf*: VI." *Anglia* 56 (1932): 436-7.

McFadden, Brian. "Sleeping after the Feast: Deathbeds, Marriage Beds, and the Power Structure of Heorot." *Neophilologus* 84 (2000): 629-646.

Mellinkoff, Ruth. "Cain's Monstrous Progeny in Beowulf: Part I, Noachic Tradition." *Anglo-Saxon England* 8 (1979): 143-62.

———. "Cain's Monstrous Progeny in *Beowulf*: Part II, Post-Diluvian Survival." *Anglo-Saxon England* 9 (1980): 183-97.

Menzer, Melinda J. "*Aglæcwif* (*Beowulf* 1259A): Implications for –*Wif* Compounds, Grendel's Mother, and Other *Aglæcan*." *English Language Notes* 34 (1996): 1-6.

Mizuno, Tomoaki. "The Magical Necklace and the Fatal Corslet in *Beowulf*." *English Studies* 80 (1999): 377-97.

Mullally, Erin. "Hrethel's Heirloom: Kinship, Succession, and Weaponry in Beowulf," in *Images of Matter: Essays on British Literature of the Middle Ages and Renaissance*, 228-44. Newark: University of Delaware Press, 2005.

Niles, John D. *Old English Heroic Poems and the Social Life of Texts*. Turnhout: Brepols, 2007.

North, Richard. "Saxo and the Swedish Wars in *Beowulf*," in *Saxo Grammaticus: Tra storiografia e letteratura*. Ed. Carlo Santini. Rome: Calamo, 1992. 175-88.

O'Brien O'Keeffe, Katherine. "*Beowulf*, Lines 702b-836: Transformations and the Limits of the Human." *Texas Studies in Literature and Language* 23 (1981): 484-94.

Orchard, Andy. *A Critical Companion to Beowulf*. Cambridge: D.S. Brewer, 2003.

———. *Pride and Prodigies: Studies in the Monsters of the* Beowulf-*Manuscript*. Toronto: University of Toronto Press, 2003.

Oswald, Dana M. "'Wigge under Wætere': Beowulf's Revision of the Fight with Grendel's Mother." *Exemplaria* 21 (2009): 63-82.

Pakis, Valentine Anthony. "The Meaning of Æschere's Name in *Beowulf.*" *Anglia* 126 (2008): 104-13.

Pearce, T.M. "*Beowulf* and the Southern Sun." *American Notes & Queries* 4 (1966): 67-8.

Roberts, Jane. "Hrothgar's 'Admirable Courage,'" in *Unlocking the Wordhord: Anglo-Saxon Studies in Memory of Edward B. Irving, Jr.*, 240-51. Mark C. Amodio and Katherine O'Brien O'Keeffe, eds. Toronto: University of Toronto Press, 2003.

Robinson, Fred C. *The Tomb of Beowulf and Other Essays on Old English*. Oxford: Blackwell, 1993.

Rosier, James L. "Design for Treachery: The Unferth Intrigue." *PMLA* 77 (1962): 1-7.

Thayer, James D. "Fractured Wisdom: The Gnomes of *Beowulf.*" *English Language Notes*. 41 (2003): 1-18.

Tolkien, J.R.R. "*Beowulf*: The Monsters and the Critics." *Proceedings of the British Academy* 22 (1936): 245-95.

Vickrey, John F. *Beowulf and the Illusion of History*. Bethlehem: Lehigh University Press, 2009.

Whitbread, L. "The Hand of Æschere: A Note on *Beowulf* 1343." *Review of English Studies* 25 (1949): 339-42.

Acknowledgments

We would like to thank Grinnell College for funding the Mentored Advanced Project and the continued work on the edition. Funding for the first print edition was provided by Grinnell's Student Publications and Radio Committee (SPARC). Much thanks to Richard Fyffe, Phil Jones, Mark McFate, Julia Bauder, Jieun Kang, Cecilia Knight, Becky Yoose, and Sheryl Bissen for publishing the edition through Digital Grinnell. Also thanks to Lena Parkhurst and Sarah Sarber, co-chairs of Grinnell Press, for their guidance and support when putting together the first printing. Heather Lobban-Viravong and Mark Schneider have supported the project from its early stages, securing funding for multiple printings and ensuring that the work could reach a wider audience. We are grateful to Marna Montgomery and Lisa Mulholland for their logistical and emotional support during our long summer of translation. Thanks to Linda Brant, Emily Whitman, and Steele Nowlin for reading early drafts of the translation. Also, thanks to Carolyn Jacobson and James Lee for providing valuable feedback in the crucial final stages of revising the poem and its notes. Dean Bakopoulos helped shape the Professor's Introduction. Elizabeth Dobbs and Paula Smith provided valuable expertise and encouragement. Finally, thanks to Dragon Wagon BBQ, whose food sustained us through our battles.

Emily Johnson, Logan Shearer, Aniela Wendt, Eva Dawson, Tim Arner, Jeanette Miller, Kate Whitman

Eva Dawson, Emily Johnson, Jeanette Miller, Logan Shearer, Aniela Wendt, Kate Whitman are members of the Grinnell College class of 2014. Tim Arner is an Associate Professor of English.

"No man, friend or enemy, could have dissuaded you / from this perilous journey when you dove / into the water."

Caleb Neubauer '13 completed most of the ink wash, charcoal, and conté crayon illustrations at the Grin City artist residency. He would like to thank the Beowulf crew for their patience and enthusiasm—it had been quite a while since he'd been asked to draw a dragon. More of his work can be seen at calebneubauer.wordpress.com.